you and your prostate

LEE RODWELL

SELF-HELP DIRECT

I would like to thank all the doctors, patients and campaigners who gave up their time to talk to me or read my manuscript, especially Tony Kilmister of the Prostate Research Campaign UK, Philip Dunn of the Prostate Help Association, Roger Kirby, consultant urologist at St George's Hospital, London and Andrew Doble, consultant urologist at Addenbrooke's NHS Trust, Cambridge

More copies of this book are available from Self-Help Direct Publishing, PO Box 9035, London, N12 8ED. Price: £10.95 cheque or postal order (postage & packing free) (overseas sales $25 per book) payable to *Self-Help Direct*. Bulk order prices on application.

Our promise: If you are not satisfied with any of our books, we will refund your money if you return the book in good condition within 10 days

DESIGN: Michael Crozier/Design Unlimited
COVER ILLUSTRATION: Michael Daley
GRAPHICS: Michael Roscoe

Published by Self-Help Direct Publishing, PO Box, London, N12 8ED
First edition 1997

ISBN 1 900461 15 3

contents

foreword

I am delighted to have this opportunity to commend *You and Your Prostate*. Lee Rodwell has consulted widely and has produced a valuable and most welcome resource. One man in two can expect to be troubled by his prostate eventually - assuming he lives beyond middle age. Yet according to a MORI poll, 89% of men do not even know where their prostate gland is. Men *should* know, as should the women who love them.

Despite their prevalence, prostate disorders have been a Cinderella, so far as the funding of scientific and medical research is concerned.

For this very good reason, Prostate Research Campaign was registered as a charity in 1994, with the aim of promoting and financing research (wherein lies hope for the future), as well as providing patient information of a high quality, yet easy to understand. Other charities in the prostate field have entered the fray, also, and details of these are listed helpfully in these pages.

The need to step up the funding of research is undeniable and urgent. I can only tell of our activity, but all research, wherever undertaken, is of the greatest importance. At the Prostate Research Campaign, we are not placing all our eggs in one basket, but want to encourage exciting new projects of quality, irrespective of their location.

For example, our first Research fellowship was at the University of Edinburgh, but more recent awards have been made to research teams at Nottingham, Leeds, Manchester and Glasgow, quite apart from a couple of grants for equipment needed by the cancer genetics team at the Royal Marsden Hospital on the outskirts of London.

Surgery is always an option, but the drive is on to develop new, effective drugs and less invasive therapies. You and Your Prostate draws a balanced picture and this book will be a boon to patients and families. There is a hunger for such information in laymen's language and this book helps satisfy that appetite.

We all recall scenes from the hugely popular and often repeated television series, Dad's Army, when Private Godfrey would yet again raise his hand and ask to "be excused". In the real world of today such problems have been revolutionised. This book tells how. So read on!

Anthony Kilmister, Founder, Prostate Research Campaign UK

introduction

The prostate gland can be thought of as a time-bomb ticking away in male plumbing. Put it another way. Having trouble with your prostate is almost as inevitable as death and taxes. This is not scaremongering: the World Health Organisation estimates that eight out of 10 men will eventually need treatment for prostate problems and, of these, one in three will need an operation.

In the United Kingdom around 100,000 new cases of prostate disorders are diagnosed each year. Of these, around 78,000 involve non-cancerous enlargement of the prostate, while about 14,000 are cases of prostate cancer. Yet despite the prevalence of prostate problems, few men know exactly where their prostate is, what it does, or what to look out for when things start to go wrong.

Most people assume that prostate problems only affect older men. This is not true. Prostatitis, for example, which is caused by inflammation or infection of the prostate gland, can affect men of any age.

Enlargement of the prostate seems to be part of the natural process of ageing which can cause symptoms in around 45 to 50 per cent of men in their sixties. Prostate cancer, too, has traditionally been seen as a disease of elderly men because very few cases occur in men under 50 and the risk of developing it rises with age.

However, while it is true that half of all prostate cancers occur in men over the age of 75, it is equally true that half of all prostate cancers occur in younger men. And when men in their fifties and sixties are getting prostate cancer, it can no longer be dismissed as an old man's disease.

In any case, no matter what age you are, forewarned is forearmed. Research indicates that many men endure the symptoms of prostate problems, rather than talk to their doctor. Instead of getting help as soon as possible, many are treated only when they develop acute health problems or their symptoms become unbearable. Yet seeking help promptly could have a significant effect on the outcome, because it means that treatment can begin at an earlier stage.

The aim of this book is to explain what the prostate is, what kind of problems can develop and how you can take steps to prevent these. It will also help you decide when and how to seek help if things start going wrong. It will explain the treatments available and explore the possible side-effects or post-operative complications so that you can weigh up the choices open to you.

It will deal frankly with the effect that some treatments can have on potency and continence, and suggest ways in which these problems can be dealt with to minimise their impact on your social life and your sexual relationship.

Above all, it aims to give you the information and confidence you need to take part in making decisions which affect your health and well-being.

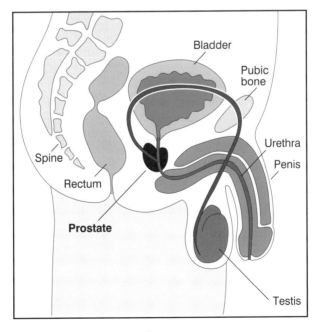

CHAPTER ONE

The prostate and its disorders: a summary

what is the prostate?

The prostate gland is about the size and shape of a walnut and is partially enclosed in a capsule of muscle and connective tissue. It is part of the male reproductive system and produces secretions which form part of the seminal fluid released in an ejaculation. These secretions help nourish the sperm and aid fertility.

When you reach orgasm, sperm from the testes and secretions from the seminal vesicles behind the bladder are carried along the ejaculatory ducts, entering the part of the urethra which is inside the prostate. Here, they mix with prostatic fluid and the mixture – semen – is then ejaculated along the urethra and out through the penis by rhythmic muscle contractions.

The prostate consists of three different zones: a central zone, a peripheral zone and a transition zone. *(diagram 1)*

Different diseases tend to affect different parts of the prostate. For instance, about four-fifths of prostate cancers originally develop in the peripheral zone. Enlargement of the prostate (benign prostatic hyperplasia or BPH) develops in the transition zone, which is why it can constrict the urethra and make urination difficult.

where is it?

The prostate sits below your bladder and above the base of your penis, between your pubic bone and your rectum. Because it encircles the urethra, urine passes through the prostate on its way out of your body.

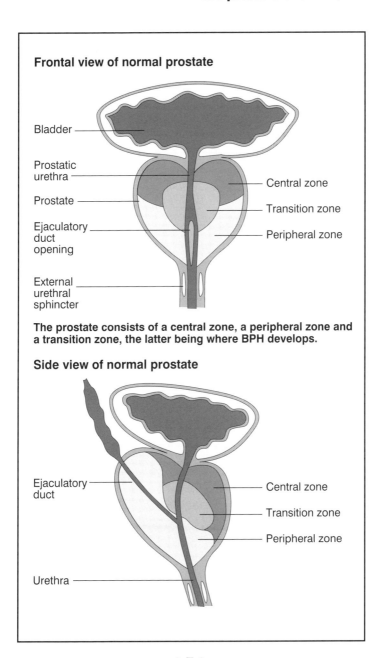

Frontal view of normal prostate

Bladder

Prostatic urethra

Prostate

Ejaculatory duct opening

External urethral sphincter

Central zone

Transition zone

Peripheral zone

The prostate consists of a central zone, a peripheral zone and a transition zone, the latter being where BPH develops.

Side view of normal prostate

Ejaculatory duct

Urethra

Central zone

Transition zone

Peripheral zone

how it develops

In newborn boys the prostate is about the size of a pea and it grows very slowly until puberty. Then there is a dramatic growth spurt and the prostate can double in size in six to 12 months. After that, growth slows, then stops. The prostate stays about the same walnut-size until a man reaches his forties, when it increases again.

This is because the growth and function of the prostate are ruled by the interaction of various hormones – primarily the male sex hormone, testosterone. This hormone is responsible for the development and function of the reproductive organs and other male characteristics, such as your voice breaking at puberty.

In the prostate, testosterone is converted to dihydrotestosterone (DHT) a more active form. DHT is responsible for the growth of the prostate. The conversion of testosterone to DHT is controlled by an enzyme known as 5-alpha reductase. In older men this hormonal regulation tends to break down, and, as a result, the prostate gets bigger.

what can go wrong?

The most common sign that you have started to develop a problem is difficulty in passing urine. This is because changes in the prostate can cause a narrowing of the urethra, the tube inside the penis through which urine passes from the bladder.

There are three conditions which commonly affect the prostate gland. They are:

◆ *prostatitis – inflammation or infection of the prostate*
This can affect men at any age of their adult life, but is not a life-threatening condition. Prostatitis can either be bacterial or non-bacterial (also referred to as abacterial prostatitis). As the names suggest, bacterial prostatitis is caused by bacteria, whereas with non-bacterial prostatitis, no bacteria are found to be present. Bacterial prostatitis may be acute (i.e. it comes on suddenly and usually lasts only a short time) or chronic (i.e .the symptoms persist or flare-up repeatedly over a period of time).

Prostatodynia means prostate pain. Although its symptoms are similar to non-bacterial prostatitis, its cause is often difficult to identify.

◆ *benign prostatic hyperplasia (BPH) – non-cancerous enlargement of the prostate*
The gradual enlargement of the prostate gland in middle-aged men can cause problems by constricting the urethra and interfering with urination. BPH is most common in men over 50. About half of all men will have BPH by the age of 60, rising to eight out of 10 in their eighties.

◆ *prostate cancer*
This is rare before middle age, with very few cases occurring in men under fifty. Half of all cases occur in men aged under 75, half in men who are over 75. Overall, the average lifetime risk of getting prostate cancer is about one in twelve. Most prostate cancers are slow growing and many can be treated effectively, especially if caught early.

Waterworks Quiz* - Should You See a Doctor?

When you want to pass water, is there a delay before you start?
A   no
B   sometimes
C   usually

When you are passing water, do you find that the flow stops and starts?
A   no
B   sometimes
C   usually

When you think you've finished, do you ever find a bit more urine trickles out and sometimes stains your underwear?
A   never
B   sometimes
C   usually

Has your urine stream become smaller or weaker in force in the last year?
A   not really
B   yes, a bit
C   yes, a lot

Do you feel your bladder is not quite empty after you've passed water?
A   never
B   sometimes
C   usually

How many times do you usually have to get up in the night to pass water?
A   never
B   1-3 times
C   4 times or more

How many times do you usually pass water during the day?
A   3-4 times
B   5-6 times
C   7 times or more

When you feel you want to pass water, do you feel you have to go straight away?
A   never
B   sometimes
C   usually

Do you ever pass water when you don't mean to?
A   never
B   sometimes
C   often

What does your score mean?

All A's: This suggests you have no difficulty in passing water.

Mainly B's: You appear to have regular difficulty in passing water, which means you always need to be able to get to a toilet easily. Your doctor will be able to help you relieve this problem.

Mainly C's: Any answers where you have selected C suggest that you have considerable difficulty in passing water. It would be advisable for you to seek help from your doctor as soon as possible.

Source: Better Prostate Health Campaign

CHAPTER TWO
....

investigating a problem

For most men the first sign that something is wrong with their prostate is having difficulty with urinating. The most common symptoms include:

◆ intermittency - a weak flow which sometimes stops and starts
◆ hesitancy - having to wait before you start to go
◆ frequency - having to urinate more often than previously
◆ urgency - finding it difficult to postpone urination
◆ nocturia - having to get up at night to urinate

Many men ignore these symptoms, believing that they are an inevitable part of the aging process. Others seek help only when the symptoms have become so marked that they interfere with the quality of their lives. They may have difficulty getting a good night's sleep. They may feel unable to continue to play sport. They may curtail their social activities because they need to be close to a lavatory at all times.

Others may feel embarrassed at discussing these matters with a doctor, or dread the prospect of examinations and tests. Or they may assume that the only treatment will involve surgery.

However, it makes sense to seek help as soon as possible since prostate disorders do not get better on their own. If an enlarged prostate has been pressing on the urethra for a long time, for instance, the back pressure of urine can eventually damage the bladder and may even affect the kidneys. Bladder stones may form; the bladder wall may get thicker and more irritable; pouches called diverticulae may form at weak points in the bladder wall.

Eventually an enlarging prostate may block the urethra completely so that urine cannot be passed at all. If this happens, you would have to be admitted to hospital so that a catheter could be inserted into the bladder to drain off the urine. Subsequently, an operation to relieve the blockage would normally be necessary. However, if the condition had been treated at an earlier stage, when symptoms were still mild to moderate, drug treatment alone might well have been effective.

A variety of tests are used to determine the cause of prostate problems. Sometimes a GP can diagnose a specific problem from a patient's symptoms, physical examinations and blood tests. Sometimes, a patient will be referred to a urologist for more extensive tests.

Initially, your doctor will ask you about the history of your problem before carrying out a physical examination including a digital rectal examination, often referred to as a DRE.

By inserting a lubricated, gloved finger gently into the rectum, a doctor can feel the prostate gland. He will be able to judge how big it seems, how mobile it is, and whether its consistency feels normal. A "boggy" and tender prostate, for instance, may suggest prostatitis. A hard or "woody" prostate, or one that contains a nodule, may indicate cancer.

A GP might use various scoring systems to measure how severe the symptoms are and he will also take a detailed medical history to rule out other possible causes of the symptoms.

Blood and urine samples will be taken for various tests. These may include a creatinine test to assess kidney function and a blood count to check for infection. Another important test is measuring the level of a protein known as prostate specific antigen (PSA) in the blood.

Low levels of PSA are present in all men, but levels may be higher in men with an enlarged prostate (BPH) or prostate cancer. Although the PSA test does not actually diagnose cancer, it does help to estimate the chance of cancer being present.

If your doctor suspects prostatitis, he may massage the prostate in order to be able to collect prostatic secretions which can be cultured to determine whether bacteria are present.

Another test, which is usually carried out at a hospital "flow" clinic is called uroflowmetry, and, as the name suggests, measures the rates of urine flow. You have to urinate into a special device which is fitted with a flow meter. This measures the time taken to urinate and the maximum and average urine flow rates.

You may also be given an ultrasound scan. A scanning device is passed over your lower body. High-frequency sound waves are reflected back like an echo and processed by a computer to build up an image which is shown on a screen. This shows whether your prostate is enlarged or abnormal, and whether any urine has been left in your bladder after urination. This test is similar to the kind given to pregnant women and is not painful or unpleasant.

There are a number of other tests which may be used if the urologist feels they are necessary. Urodynamics also measures the urine flow rate and pressure but, as this involves the insertion of a small catheter and can be uncomfortable, is mainly used where other tests have given confusing results.

If a urologist thinks there is a possibility that cancer is present, he may ask you to have transrectal ultrasound scanning (TRUS). An ultrasound probe is inserted into the rectum to take pictures of the prostate and its surroundings. A prostate biopsy is often taken at the same time to obtain tissue from the prostate which can then be tested to detect or exclude prostate cancer.

This can be done by passing a spring-loaded needle down a special channel alongside the ultra-sound probe. The procedure is uncomfortable but not painful, although a needle prick may be felt when each biopsy is performed. Four to six samples of tissue are usually taken at one time.

Because there is a risk of infection, patients are given antibiotics before and after the test. Even so, it is still possible for infection to develop: if a patient starts running a temperature after a biopsy, his doctor should be called.

You should also be aware that, as the tissue of the prostate gland has been cut, there may be blood in your bowel motions and urine for a day or so and your semen may also contain blood for some time.

Intravenous urography (also known as pyelography) is sometimes used to examine the workings of the entire urinary tract. A radioactive dye is injected into a vein in your arm so that it can work its way through your system. After an hour or so it will start to be excreted by your kidneys and passed through your bladder. A series of X-rays are taken to record what happens.

Computerised tomography (CT scanning) and magnetic resonance imaging (MRI) are two types of body scans. They are sometimes used to see how far prostate cancer has advanced and whether it has spread.

With CT you are given a drink and an injection of a contrast agent. You then lie on a table which passes through a hoop-shaped scanner while X-rays are taken. These are interpreted by a computer.

With MRI, you lie inside a large, hollow cylindrical magnet. However, some patients find the tunnel makes them feel claustrophobic and MRI cannot be used if you have a pacemaker, a hip replacement or any other implant containing metal.

If prostate cancer is diagnosed, an isotope bone scan may be done to detect any secondary tumours in your skeleton.

Depending on your test results and a variety of other factors, such as the severity of your symptoms, your age and general state of health, your doctor will recommend a course of treatment for your problem. Remember, the final decision to have a particular treatment is yours. You may wish for time to consider, to discuss things with your partner or other members of your family.

There may be things you feel you have not fully understood. You need to be sure you understand any possible side-effects relating to any treatment which is being recommended. If you need any further explanations, do not be afraid to ask if there is someone you can talk to. You may also wish to get in touch with one of the self-help organisations listed on page 102.

CHAPTER THREE

prostatitis

The prostate consists of millions of tiny glands which can become infected, inflamed or clogged, causing a condition called prostatitis. Signs to watch out for include pain, needing to urinate more frequently than usual, and experiencing difficulties when passing urine. If you begin to experience any of these symptoms you should seek help from your doctor as soon as possible.

Doctors recognise three types of prostatitis: acute and chronic bacterial prostatitis; nonbacterial prostatitis; and prostatodynia. It is important to find out which kind you are suffering from, as only then will your doctor be able to decide on the best form of treatment or management of your symptoms.

acute bacterial prostatitis

This is usually caused by the bacteria responsible for urinary tract infections, resident in the bowel. These get into the urinary system either through the urethra or by travelling in the bloodstream or lymphatic fluids.

An attack comes on suddenly and symptoms may include:
- feeling unwell
- fever or chills
- low back pain
- aching round the thighs and genitals
- deep pain between the scrotum and anus
- urinary problems such as pain and difficulty on passing water
- frequency of passing water
- pain on ejaculation

chronic bacterial prostatitis

This is the term given to recurrent or persistent bouts of prostatitis, caused by bacteria. The most common organism is Escherichia coli, which accounts for eight out of 10 cases. When the prostate gland becomes infected it swells and this may block the normal drainage channels. As a result, bacteria may be trapped in the prostate. Sometimes, bacteria become coated in secretions which harden to form tiny crystals, making them resistant to antibiotics or the body's own immune system. This is why some men experience repeated flare-ups of bacterial prostatitis.

Symptoms can vary but often include:
- aching in the lower back, lower abdomen or thighs
- pain and discomfort between scrotum and anus
- urinary problems such as pain on passing water
- frequency or urgency in passing water
- pain on ejaculation
- premature ejaculation
- blood in the semen
- pain and swelling in the testes
- watery discharge from the penis

chronic non-bacterial prostatitis
Sometimes the prostate becomes inflamed although there are no bacteria present. However, research has shown that men with chronic non-bacterial prostatitis have antibodies within the prostate. Antibodies neutralise antigens, substances which trigger the immune response. This indicates some kind of organism is present – but what? Current evidence suggests that although the persistent irritant is not bacteria, it may be the remnants of bacteria such as bacterial walls.

Another possibility may be that some men are more prone than others to reflux urine. The urethra passes through the prostate. If the muscle below the prostate is not completely relaxed during urination, this may lead to urine being forced back into the channels that drain the prostate since they have no valves to stop this happening.

Andrew Doble, consultant urologist at Addenbrooke's NHS Trust,

Cambridge, says: "Could it be that we all reflux urine into our prostates? If an organism is 'washed in with the tide', then chronic bacterial prostatitis develops. But if another antigen, yet to be determined, is deposited in the prostate, then chronic non-bacterial prostatitis develops."

Another theory is that the prostate secretions produced by some men are thicker or possibly more acid than normal. These do not drain away so easily and build up to cause the swelling and irritation.

Symptoms include:
♦ aches or pain in the testicle, penis or rectum
♦ low backache, especially after sex
♦ urinary problems such as pain or burning on passing water
♦ frequency of passing water
♦ discharge from the penis

prostatodynia
This can be even more of a mystery than chronic non-bacterial prostatitis. Sufferers experience the same kind of pain and symptoms as men with prostatitis, but tests show no sign of infection or inflammation. Even prostate secretions look normal.

Because of this, some doctors have suggested this is a psychosexual problem. However, other believe there is probably a physical cause, such as spasm of the pelvic floor muscles.

It may also be that prostatodynia is a chemical irritation of the prostatic ducts caused by intra-prostatic urinary reflux, explained above.

Symptoms may include:
♦ pain on ejaculation or erection
♦ perineal discomfort on sitting
♦ burning on passing water

investigation and treatment
Your doctor may decide to refer you to a specialist in urology or

genito-urinary medicine. In any event, you will be given a genital examination so the doctor can check whether there is any discharge from the end of your penis and whether you have signs of inflammation, such as redness or soreness.

You may also be given a rectal examination. By inserting a finger into your back passage your doctor can assess the size and texture of your prostate gland. Many men dislike the idea of this, or feel embarrassed at the thought, and put off going to see the doctor as a result.

However, digital rectal examination (DRE) is a routine procedure. There is no reason to feel any more embarrassed than if a doctor was examining the glands on your neck; your doctor will be just as matter-of-fact about it. Besides, a DRE is not as unpleasant as many men fear.

The doctor wears gloves and uses a water-based jelly as a lubricant. Only the index finger is inserted, which, after all, is much thinner than the width of the average bowel motion.

Other tests may also be done. Swabs may be taken by inserting a sterile cotton bud into the end of the penis to collect any discharge. These can be checked for the presence of bacteria or any other infection such as chlamydia, a micro-organism which shares some of the characteristics of both bacteria and viruses.

You may also be given a blood test, as a raised white cell count indicates an infection is present. A urine sample may be sent off for testing or a "three-glass" urine test may be carried out to try to pin-point the site of any possible infection.

If so, you will be asked to provide samples by passing a small amount of urine into one jar and more into a second. Before you have emptied your bladder completely, you are asked to stop. The doctor then gently massages your prostate gland by inserting a gloved finger into your rectum.

This releases secretions which can be collected at the end of the penis. If no fluid appears you will be asked to pass a small sample of urine into a third glass jar to flush these secretions through.

The first two urine samples will be checked for cloudiness and signs of protein or blood. Any threads of cellular material will be taken out for examination under a microscope as the presence of bacteria or pus cells can help diagnosis. All the samples will then be sent off to a laboratory where they will be tested to see if they contain bacteria.

As the table below indicates, the results can aid diagnosis.

Results	Indicates
Bacteria found in first sample	Infection of the urethra
Bacteria found in second sample	Bladder infection
More bacteria in third sample than first	Prostatitis
Pus cells but no significant bacteria	Non-bacterial prostatitis
No bacteria, very few pus cells	Prostatodynia

If your doctor diagnoses acute bacterial prostatitis you will be given a course of antibiotics. You will probably have to take these for at least four weeks. Your symptoms should start to improve within a few days, but you should continue to the end of the prescribed course to make sure you are clear of all infection.

Sometimes infection causes so much swelling that the urethra is squeezed shut and urination is impossible. In these circumstances you would be admitted to hospital to have a catheter temporarily inserted into the bladder under local anaesthetic to ease the flow.

Chronic bacterial prostatitis can be more difficult to treat and a longer course of antibiotics – three months or more – is generally required. Taking anti-inflammatory painkillers, such as ibuprofen, may help reduce swelling, pain and inflammation.

Chronic non-bacterial prostatitis can be difficult to clear up completely although a long course of antibiotics may be successful. Some sufferers have been helped by a natural food supplement derived from rye pollen extracts which can help reduce swelling, irritation and inflammation.

Prostatodynia is also difficult to treat because it is not easy to identify the cause of the problem. Some studies suggest that pain can be relieved by microwave hyperthermia. This means using a special instrument, inserted into the back passage, to warm the prostate, increasing the blood supply to the area and speeding up the body's own healing powers. Other treatments which have been tried include the use of muscle relaxant and anti-spasmodic drugs.

less conventional treatments
Philip Dunn, Secretary of the Prostate Help Association, says it is not uncommon for men to be told there is nothing wrong with them, or to be diagnosed as having prostatodynia or non-bacterial prostatitis when, in fact, there may be bacteria present.

"Imagine the segment of an orange. Inside that segment are hundreds of smaller tear-shaped pieces. Those are like the smaller glands inside the prostate gland. Now imagine bacteria sealed inside one of those smaller glands – the chances of finding it are likely to be very slim."

In the past, prostate massage was quite commonly carried out to relieve the symptoms of pain, but in the UK this practice has gone out of fashion. However, Dr Antonio Feliciano, a doctor from the Philippines who specialises in prostatitis, uses massage as part of his treatment to drain the prostate and allow the appropriate antibiotic to reach the bacteria.

Precise details of this procedure are available from the Prostate Help Association. However, Mr Dunn points out that to his knowledge there have been no independent clinical trials showing whether this method works or not, although there is anecdotal evidence from patients who say they were helped. Moreover, even if you found a doctor prepared to carry out the massage (which has to be done every two days), the cost of treatment and of sending specimens off for laboratory testing would probably be prohibitive.

Another possible treatment prostatitis sufferers have been talking about amongst themselves is allopurinol. Allopurinol is usually prescribed as a treatment for gout because it reduces the levels of uric acid in the blood. However, some men have tried it for prostatitis.

● Mr E, a 56-year-old suffering from chronic non-bacterial prostatitis for 15 years, had a trans-rectal ultrasound. This showed he had a number of stones which he had read could be storehouses for bacteria. He decided to do some research and discovered that many stones have been found to be made up of the same ingredients as found in urine.

He also tracked down some Swedish research, which indicated that urine refluxing into the prostatic ducts could cause prostatitis in some men. These men were prescribed allopurinol. Half the group were given 300mg a day, the other half 600mg.

When Mr E approached his urologist he warned him allopurinol was a potent drug, but agreed to go ahead with 300mg a day. After two weeks, Mr E obtained a further alternative supply and treated himself with 600mg every other day.

Several weeks later he reported that his symptoms were almost gone. He was free of sitting pain, pain in his left thigh and testicle, pain on urination, pain the morning after sex. Even pain on ejaculation was down by fifty per cent. He no longer had symptoms of urgency or frequency and he was only having to get up once in the night to urinate, instead of three to five times.

● Mr C had been suffering from non-bacterial prostatitis for nearly a year. Antibiotics had no effect; alpha-blockers made him dizzy; natural remedies such as zinc, pumpkin seeds and cranberries had had no effect. Then he did a Worldwide Web search on his computer for prostatitis and read about Mr E and his allopurinol research. Armed with this information he saw his specialist who said that the drug had not been approved for treatment of prostatitis in the UK. However, he agreed to "give it a go" with Mr C's consent. After taking 300mg daily for three and a half weeks, Mr C reported that he was feeling optimistic and his symptoms did seem to be improving.

Of course, two swallows don't make a summer and the Prostate Help Association knows of men who have tried allopurinol and found no improvement. There is also some evidence to suggest that the effects can wane after a period of about three months. In addition, allopurinol may cause side effects including rashes, itching, nausea, vertigo and drowsiness.

On top of this, in an article published in the Lancet in 1996, *Allopurinol for prostatitis: where is the evidence?* the Canadian authors argued that an examination of the published data indicated that adopting this therapy was premature. They criticised the Swedish study on a number of points, saying that there was no real evidence (except for a non-validated questionnaire) that the patients did have non-bacterial prostatitis and concluded:

"Chronic non-bacterial prostatitis remains a confusing and frustrating clinical enigma for physicians and patients. Any encouraging therapy for chronic non-bacterial prostatitis must be rigorously and prospectively tried in a well-defined group of prostatitis patients and must be compared with a similar placebo group by means of both objective and subjective analysis . . .

"Symptom evaluation must be more than a single statement of how the patient rates his entire symptom complex or how much pain the examiner perceives the patient is experiencing during his prostate examination, and it must based on validated symptom questionnaires."

prevention and self-help
Since prostatitis can occasionally be caused by organisms which also cause sexually-transmitted diseases, it makes sense to use a condom

if you are likely to be at any risk. If you are suffering from prostatitis it may be advisable to abstain from intercourse while you have symptoms or are being treated. If you have an infection, there is a risk of passing this on to a female partner, causing cystitis or a vaginal infection. Your doctor will be able to advise you about this, so don't be afraid to raise the subject.

For pain relief, doctors usually recommend taking painkillers which also have an anti-inflammatory effect. These include aspirin and ibuprofen. Sitting in a hot bath may also provide relief and help reduce swelling.

You might also want to consider your diet and lifestyle. For instance, regular exercise and a high-fibre diet help keep the bowels open. This is important if you suffer from prostatodynia, especially if you spend most of the day sitting at a desk or behind the wheel of a car. Sitting and constipation can both increase congestion in the prostate.

Try to make a note of anything in your normal diet, such as spicy foods, which seem to trigger a recurrence of your symptoms. Nicotine, alcohol and caffeine may set off attacks of pain. Stress may also make things worse. You may find it helpful to try some relaxation techniques. Most libraries have a selection of books and tapes on this subject.

Some sufferers report their symptoms have been relieved by taking a teaspoon of bicarbonate of soda in a glass of water each morning, although this can have the side-effect of loosening the bowels.

Natural therapists often suggest zinc supplements may help to relieve the symptoms of non-bacterial prostatitis. They recommend taking supplements in the form of zinc picolinate. Sunflower and pumpkin seeds are also rich sources of zinc. Vitamin B6 supplements may help the body to absorb zinc.

Rye pollen tablets and cranberry tablets can have an anti-inflammatory effect. One study, published in the British Journal of

Urology in 1989, attempted to evaluate the efficacy of plant pollen extracts in the treatment of patients with chronic non-bacterial prostatitis and prostatodynia.

Fifteen patients took part and the duration of treatment with the extract varied from one to 18 months. Seven patients became symptom-free, six were significantly improved and two failed to respond. Most patients did not begin to show any signs of improvement in signs or symptoms until three months after starting treatment. Another study, published in the same journal in 1993, involving ninety patients, also had encouraging results.

The pollen extract used, Cernilton, is available in the UK as ProstaBrit. This is a herbal supplement containing an extract of natural Swedish rye grass plants and is available at health stores and chemists.

Prostate Help Association
Langworth, Lincoln, LN3 5DF
Can supply information on all prostate problems, including prostatitis. For initial information sheet, send two first class stamps.

Prostate Research Campaign UK
36, The Drive, Northwood, Middlesex HA6 1HP
Send a 9 x 7 inch sae for information and free fact sheets, including one on prostatitis.

CHAPTER FOUR
....
benign prostatic hyperplasia (BPH)

Benign prostatic hyperplasia – a non-cancerous enlargement of the prostate gland – is common in many older men. It is rarely a life-threatening condition and only occasionally gives rise to serious problems such as urinary retention or kidney disorders.

Nevertheless, the symptoms of an enlarged prostate – having to pass urine frequently, having to get up during the night and so on – can be difficult to cope with and may become so troublesome that they seriously affect the sufferer's quality of life.

A basic design flaw in the male body means that the urethra passes through the prostate. So, if the prostate starts to enlarge, the flow of urine through the urethra can be restricted – leading to a range of bothersome and distressing difficulties with urination.

In theory, any older man may develop BPH – the only clearly defined risk factors are having reached middle age and being in possession of functioning testes. It has been reported that clinical BPH is more common in black races than white ones, but further studies have yet to confirm this.

Asian races appear to have lower incidence rates than white races. In addition, there is some evidence that Asians who migrate to the West increase their risk of developing BPH. This suggests that dietary or environmental factors, as well as genetic ones, may be involved.

BPH has also been reported to be less common in men who eat large amounts of vegetables. This might account for the differences in the incidence rates of BPH in the East and the West, although it has yet to be proved.

There is certainly a tendency for BPH to run in families. If one of your first-degree relatives has had problems with BPH, then you are at greater risk yourself of suffering the same kind of trouble.

But what causes the prostate to start enlarging once a man reaches his later years? There are a number of theories. Androgens are a group of hormones which cause the development of male secondary sexual characteristics. One is these is testosterone. Testosterone, produced by the testes, enters the prostate where it reacts in the cells with an enzyme, 5-alpha reductase, becoming the more potent androgen, dihydrotestosterone (DHT). The DHT then binds to androgen receptors in the nucleus of the cells, thus promoting cell growth.

One theory suggests that the cells in the prostate gradually become more sensitive to androgens with aging. Another suggests that enlargement may be linked to an imbalance between oestrogen and testosterone. Although oestrogens are usually thought of as women's hormones, men produce small amounts of oestrogen in the adrenal glands. Testosterone levels decrease gradually with age while the circulating level of free oestradiol stays the same. It may be that oestrogens sensitise the prostate to androgens. Yet another theory suggests that BPH develops as a result of an imbalance between cell proliferation and cell death. The more researchers find out, the more, it seems, there is to know. Clearly, the cause of BPH is complex. However, most men will inevitably be less interested in why they have developed the problem, than how to deal with it. Even then, there is no simple answer.

The prostate is made up of three distinct zones: a central zone, a peripheral zone and a transition zone which surrounds the urethra. BPH develops in this transitional zone which is why it can cause problems with urination.

Surprisingly, experts say there is little correlation between the overall size of the prostate and the degree to which the outflow of urine is likely to be obstructed. Moreover, BPH usually progresses slowly, yet this progression does not always go hand in hand with a worsening of symptoms. Some men who have been experiencing problems may find their symptoms stay stable, others may find they even improve with time.

In the past, the only treatment for BPH was prostatectomy, an operation to remove all or part of the prostate. The fear of being told they might need this operation may still deter some men from seeking medical help. However, there are now many different ways of treating prostate enlargement, particularly if help is sought soon enough.

In deciding what course of treatment to suggest, your doctor will take into account the severity of your symptoms and how much they are affecting you and your life. He would also bear in mind your age and your general health.

Ideally, what you need is a treatment which is very effective yet which also has few side-effects. Unfortunately, the treatments which are best at unblocking the urethra tend to have a greater risk of side-effects than those which don't work so effectively. That is why it is important to get as much information as possible before deciding what course of action would be most appropriate for you.

so what are the possibilities?

watchful waiting
If your symptoms are still mild, or if you are not unduly bothered by them, your doctor may simply advise what is known as "watchful waiting." This means going back to see your doctor regularly, so that he can re-examine you each time to see whether the problem is getting worse or not. Not all prostates go on getting bigger.

Your doctor may also advise you on changes you can make to your lifestyle to help relieve some of the symptoms of BPH. You might, for instance, avoid drinking large volumes of liquids at any one time, or avoid drinks altogether before going to bed. You might also consider limiting your intake of drinks containing alcohol or caffeine (coffee, tea or cola), which may stimulate the bladder.

drug treatments

Mild to moderate symptoms may be treated with drugs. Two different groups of drugs are used: alpha blockers and 5-alpha reductase inhibitors.

The prostate consists mainly of two types of tissue, glandular tissue and smooth muscle. Alpha blockers relax the smooth muscle in the prostate thus relieving the pressure on the urethra. They don't affect the enlargement of the prostate, but they do provide relief from some of the symptoms. If they are going to work, they usually do so within two to three weeks.

It is thought that around 60-75% of men gain some benefit from these drugs but they can cause side effects in around one in ten patients. The most common side effects are headache, dizziness, faintness or tiredness. Alpha blockers sometimes cause problems with erections and potency. If this occurs, ask your doctor if he can prescribe another drug. Some alpha blockers also lower blood pressure, which can be a useful side effect if you suffer from hypertension.

Alpha blockers used to treat BPH include prazosin, alfuzosin, indoramin, terazosin, doxazosin and tamsulosin.

5-alpha reductase inhibitors (such as finasteride) block production of the hormone dihydrotestosterone (DHT), which is thought to be the main hormone involved in prostate enlargement. As a result, the rate at which the prostate is enlarging slows or stops and, in some cases, the prostate may actually shrink. In any event. the symptoms will not worsen and often improve.

It can take up to six months to get the best results but these drugs improve symptoms in more than half of all patients treated. The biggest drawback is that some patients find that 5-alpha reductase inhibitors can reduce sex drive and cause difficulties with getting erections. These side-effects usually disappear if treatment is stopped. However, if treatment stops, the prostate tends to enlarge again.

Finasteride, which poses a risk to pregnant women, is excreted in semen. If there is a chance of your partner getting pregnant, you should wear condoms during intercourse. Women who could get pregnant should not handle the tablets.

surgery

Many doctors still regard surgery as the most effective way of relieving the symptoms of BPH. That's why prostatectomy – removing the part of the prostate which is blocking the urethra – is usually recommended to patients whose symptoms cannot be controlled by drugs, those who have urinary tract or other complications, and those who would rather have an operation than take medication.

TURP (transurethral resection of the prostate) is often called the gold standard treatment. It is carried out under an epidural or a light general anaesthetic and usually takes less than an hour. Because the prostate can regrow, about one in 10 men may need a second operation within five years.

If you are taking warfarin for a pre-existing medical condition, you have to stop taking it four to five days before the operation. You will be given heparin intravenously, instead. If you are taking regular doses of aspirin, this should be stopped two weeks before surgery. During the operation an instrument called a resectoscope is passed through the opening at the end of the penis and along the urethra. The prostate tissue obstructing the urethra is cut away in small chips. A catheter is passed up the urethra into the bladder to drain off the urine. This is removed after 36-48 hours. You can usually go home after three or four days, but will be advised to take things quietly for a few weeks.

The flow rate usually improves rapidly after the operation but it may take a few months before the need to pass urine frequently subsides. Any urgency, or burning when passing urine, usually disappears within a short time. You may observe blood in your urine for several days, or even weeks, after the operation but normally your urine will gradually clear.

There can be complications following the operation: sometimes the bleeding which occurs as a result of the surgery is severe enough to require a blood transfusion. Secondary haemorrhaging – bleeding which may occur 10 to 14 days after the operation – is relatively common but generally minor. The treatment is usually bedrest, drinking more fluids and appropriate antibiotics. Occasionally the bleeding is severe and if clots are being retained, the patient may have to go back into hospital to be catheterised. Sometimes a bladder washout to remove the clots is necessary.

The most common after-effect of TURP is retrograde ejaculation. This happens because the neck of the bladder no longer closes properly during orgasm, so semen flows back into the bladder instead of being ejaculated through the penis. This is not harmful although the sensation of orgasm is usually different to what you have been used to. The semen comes out the next time urine is passed.

However, it does mean that you are likely to be subfertile and if you think you might want to father more children in the future, you could consider having sperm samples frozen and stored in a sperm bank before the operation. The Human Fertilisation and Embryology Authority in London can supply a list of sperm banks, but you would then have to contact individual clinics to see if they offered this service and how much it might cost. Other sources of information may be ISSUE, the National Fertility Association, and NIAC, the National Infertility Awareness Campaign.

A significant number of men report erection difficulties after the operation, although urologists argue that there is no obvious surgical explanation for this and point out that some cases may be psychological or simply a result of aging.

There is also a slight risk of incontinence. Urge incontinence is the most likely, but usually disappears within a few months. It can be treated with anticholinergic drugs which relax the muscles of the bladder.

Occasionally patients experience stress incontinence, due to some degree of damage to the sphincter. If this is still a worrying problem after six months, an operation to put in an artificial urinary sphincter may be necessary.

Another complication, which occurs in up to five to six per cent of cases is urethral stricture. This means that part of the urethra has become narrower following surgery and as a result is restricting the flow of urine. Urethral strictures most commonly show up about four or five months after the TURP and a return to all those urination problems can be very disappointing.

Although these possible complications may sound off-putting, urologists point out that TURP provides greater improvements in symptoms and urine flow rates than any other treatment currently available. They argue that most patients are satisfied with the outcome, although they admit that between 10 to 20 per cent may have a less than perfect result.

However, Philip Dunn, secretary of the Prostate Help Association, argues that anecdotal evidence suggests the number of men who are less than happy with the results of their TURP may be higher than many urologists believe.

TUIP (transurethral incision of the prostate) may be used where the prostate is still relatively small. Carried out under an epidural or a light general anaesthetic, the procedure takes about 15 minutes. An instrument is passed up the urethra and one or two small cuts are made in the bladder neck and prostate. This allows the prostate tissue around the urethra to spring apart, reducing the pressure and making it easier to pass urine.

The stay in hospital and the recovery time are shorter than after a TURP and complications are less likely.

Open prostatectomy is usually only done if the prostate is very large. It is carried out under general anaesthetic and usually takes about an hour. Part of the prostate is removed through a cut in the lower abdomen, which will leave a scar. Most patients can leave hospital after a week, but pain after the operation is more likely than after TURP, because of the incision. A longer convalescent period is needed and complications are slightly more common.

minimally invasive treatments

Prostatic stents are small metal coils which are inserted into the urethra to hold it open. The procedure is carried out under a light general anaesthetic and takes less than 15 minutes.

Unfortunately, although they sound the perfect answer, stents have a number of disadvantages. Both permanent and temporary stents can become encrusted with calcium salts and their presence increases the risk of urinary tract infection. Temporary stents can get displaced and have, in any case, to be replaced every six months. With permanent stents, tissue can grow through the holes in the mesh of the coil, causing obstruction once more.

As a result of these problems, stents are usually only used to treat patients with acute or chronic urinary retention, who are unfit for conventional surgery. Balloon dilation – a method of inflating a balloon in the urethra to keep it open – is rarely used these days as it did not appear to prove effective long-term.

Hyperthermia involves heating the prostate. Various devices have been developed to do this and they tend to use either microwaves or radio-frequency as a heat source, and the applicator is inserted into either the rectum (Transrectal or TR treatment) or the urethra (transurethal or TU treatment).

Transurethral microwave thermotherapy (TUMT) uses microwave energy to destroy some of the prostate tissue by heat.

A catheter containing a microwave coil is inserted into the urethra and the prostate tissue is heated to about 45–55 degrees C. A cooling system aims to ensure that heat from the coil does not damage other tissues and the temperature of other tissues is monitored by a device inserted into the rectum. The Prostatron™ has been extensively evaluated, but other units are now being investigated.

A review of many European studies on the use of thermotherapy shows that this treatment can improve symptoms in some men. However, one disadvantage is that one in four patients experience temporary urinary retention afterwards, as the damaged prostate swells before it shrinks.

Even so, since this method of treatment avoids some of the risks associated with surgery, some men may feel this is a possibility worth considering. However, in Britain, consultants tend to be less enthusiastic about the possibilities of this treatment than they used to be.

Transurethral radio-frequency (TURF) is a technology developed by Direx Systems and also known as Thermex. A thermal electrode is inserted into the urethra and the treatment uses radio-frequency energy to apply heat. This causes the cells in the prostate to die off so that it should shrink gradually over four to six weeks following treatment. Proponents of this system claim it not only avoids the problems of 'hot-spots' associated with microwave systems, but has a low incidence of side or after effects and no adverse effect on ejaculation, potency or sexual function (although patients are advised to abstain from sex for about two weeks following treatment). TURF can be done as a single session day case procedure, which does not require a general anaesthetic and patients can go home and resume their normal routine straight away.

Direx have also developed a complementary treatment, **Transurethral Ablation Prostatectomy (TURAPY)**, designed to correct obstructive BPH. Direx say that a one-hour single day-case procedure can remove a similar amount of tissue to that removed in a typical transurethral prostatectomy, but without the associated risks. A pilot study on 20 men aged between 55 and 81, carried out at the Western General Hospital in Edinburgh, found that treatment with the TURAPY device was found to be safe, feasible and effective in improving both subjective and objective measurements of BPH.

There are two permanent Thermex installations in the UK – at the Western General Hospital and another at Brighton. Mobile machines travel to other centres.

Laser therapy is another form of treatment which looks promising although it is still undergoing evaluation. A probe is inserted through the urethra and then some of the prostate tissue is destroyed by the laser. Bleeding is rare afterwards, but the treated area will feel sore and patients may experience a burning sensation when passing urine which can last for four weeks or longer. There may also be urinary infection. However, there is less risk of retrograde ejaculation or of impotence than after conventional prostate surgery.

Work goes on to find new and better ways to use heat to destroy prostate tissue that is causing the problem without destroying tissue elsewhere. Possibilities include the use of high intensity focused ultrasound.

which treatment is best for you?
Increasingly the person most likely to be giving you advice about the best form of treatment for BPH will be your GP. There is a shortage of urologists and, in any case, changes in the National Health Service are putting an increasing emphasis on the role of primary-care physicians. As a result, GPs are now expected and encouraged to provide services that you might once have expected to be referred to a specialist for.

There are some advantages to this: your GP is more likely to know you and appreciate the kinds of factors which are important to you. Being seen and treated by your GP, rather than a hospital specialist, means you won't have to spend time travelling to and waiting in hospital outpatient clinics.

However, a GP may not be up-to-date or *au fait* with the latest thinking on the management of BPH. He may, for instance, automatically suggest surgery as the solution to the problem. In some cases, of course, this may be necessary. If your urine flow is badly or completely obstructed there is a risk of infection and possible permanent kidney damage, so surgery may the best, even the only, answer.

On the other hand, BPH can be managed successfully without surgery and these days many doctors see the medical management of the condition as an option in its own right, rather than a stopgap measure for men who are waiting for an operation.

If your BPH is mild to moderate you might want to explore the possibilities of Thermex treatment on the grounds that you can resort to other means of solving your problem if it doesn't work for you. Some specialists have expressed concern about patients who try a variety of treatments, only to end up having surgery anyway. Even so, there are patients who feel it is reasonable to consider surgery only as a last resort.

The important thing is not to be rushed into a course of action unnecessarily. Do not be afraid to question your doctor. Get as much information as you can to help you make a balanced decision.

You need to take into account the severity of your symptoms and how far they interfere with your everyday life. Asking yourself some simple questions might help you make up your mind.
● If you were to spend the rest of your life with your urinary condition just the way it is now, how would you feel about it?
● Thinking back about your symptoms over the past month, how do you feel about them?
● To what extent do your symptoms stop you doing what you want to do?
● Are your symptoms bad enough for you to want to take treatment on a regular basis?
● Are they bad enough for you to consider an operation in a bid to improve them?

You also need to gather information to help you predict the likely outcome of any given course of treatment: this means asking your doctor what improvements in your symptoms you could reasonably expect, how long these improvements might reasonably be expected to last, whether you would need further treatment in future – and what kind.

You need to consider the possibility of side-effects or complications following treatment and consider how these might affect you and your life.

You need to bear in mind the kind of person you are – are you the kind who would rather avoid surgery if at all possible, or are you the kind who would rather have an operation than take regular medication?

When your doctor talks about the benefits of treatment, make sure he explains the difference between what health professionals call direct and indirect outcomes. A direct outcome is one which you will notice – an indirect outcome is one which can easily be measured by a doctor, but may be less important to you. Two examples of indirect outcomes, for instance, would be an improvement in peak flow urine rate and the volume of urine left in your bladder after urination (post-void residual volume of urine).

In the end, what you have to weigh up in your own mind is the effect of BPH on your life and the likelihood that a particular therapy will improve things in the long term, against the risks of that particular treatment.

prevention and self-help
Clearly the only things which would definitely stop you getting BPH are beyond your control: you can't change your sex and you can't stop getting older. Nor can you change your genetic inheritance. However, that doesn't mean there is nothing you can do to help prevent BPH developing or to relieve any problems if it does.

change your diet
A Japanese study has shown that the incidence of BPH is higher in men who consumed large amounts of milk than in those who ate lots of vegetables. It has been suggested that vegetables and other

elements in the Japanese diet, including soya, may give some degree of protection against developing BPH because they contain phyto-oestrogens which have anti-androgenic effects on the prostate.

The World Health Organisation guidelines on healthy eating recommend increasing our intake of fruit and vegetables, and cutting back our intake of red meat and other sources of saturated fat, so changing your diet would be good for your general health and may also be good for your prostate.

It is probably wise to reduce your consumption of alcohol and caffeine-containing drinks. Caffeine can irritate the bladder and alcohol can reduce your ability to absorb zinc.

zinc

Zinc is believed to inhibit the activity of 5-alpha reductase and has been shown to reduce the size of the prostate and the symptoms of BPH. In the United States, a team of researchers in Chicago have been studying zinc and its relation to prostate health for more than 10 years. More than 5,000 patients have been involved and the evidence suggests that zinc can not only help prevent prostate enlargement, but is important in keeping the prostate gland healthy.

Foods high in zinc include oysters, herring, clams, wheat bran and wheat germ, molasses, eggs, nuts and seeds, particularly pumpkin seeds. It seems that almost 50 years ago, researchers noted that prostate enlargement was almost non-existent in Transylvania, where pumpkin seeds are an important part of the diet!

If you are going to try taking zinc supplements, zinc picolinate and perhaps zinc citrate are the most easily absorbed. Taking a vitamin B6 supplement as well may help zinc absorption.

herbal medicines

Some patients with BPH have reported significant improvements after taking an essential fatty acid (EFA) complex containing linoleic, linolenic and arachidonic acids. You could try adding linseed, sunflower, soy or evening primrose oil to your diet, making sure you have the equivalent to four grams a day. Evening primrose oil, for example, can act as 5-alpha reductase inhibitor and has an anti-inflammatory action.

In Europe, flower pollen has been used to treat BPH since the early 1960s. Several small, double-blind studies suggest it can be quite effective and the effects may be related to the high content of plant flavenoids.

Researchers in the department of urology at the University Hospital of Wales carried out a double-blind, placebo-controlled study to evaluate the effect of a six-month course of a pollen extract in patients with outflow obstruction due to BPH.

The results were published in *The British Journal of Urology* in 1990 and the researchers concluded that the pollen extract, Cernilton (available in the UK as the health supplement ProstaBrit) has a beneficial effect in BPH and may have a place in the treatment of patients with mild or moderate symptoms of outflow obstruction.

ProstaBrit contains an extract of natural Swedish rye grass plants. However, the best known herbal remedy is saw palmetto.

saw palmetto (*serenoa repens*) is a scrubby palm tree, native to the Atlantic coast of North America from South Carolina to Florida. The deep red-brown to black berries have a well-established history of use in folk medicine as an aphrodisiac and sexual rejuvenator and have also long been used to treat conditions of the prostate.

Saw palmetto berries contain beta-sitosterol. This appears to inhibit the conversion of testosterone to the hormone DHT, thus stopping prostate enlargement and even reversing the growth.

A number of clinical studies published in the early 1980s confirmed that serenoa extract can help relieve symptoms of BPH. More recently, in June 1995, *The Lancet* carried the results of a double-blind clinical trial of beta-sitosterol in patients with BPH. It showed there had been significant improvement in symptoms and urinary flow, although no reduction of prostatic volume was noted (in other words there was no reverse of growth).

However, not all the centres taking part in the trial assessed prostatic volume, which can, in any case, be difficult to measure accurately.

There is now a range of products on the market which contain extract of saw palmetto. These include:
● Sabalin (saw palmetto extract)
● Prost-8 (saw palmetto, amino acids, zinc, bee pollen, ginseng and lycopene - a carotenoid from tomatoes)
● Solgar's saw palmetto/pygeum/lycopene complex
● Efaprost (evening primrose oil, beta-sitosterol, saw palmetto, Vitamin E)

Results of a study run in conjunction with the Prostate Health

	Watchful waiting	Alpha-blockers	5-alpha reductase inhibitors	TURP	TUIP	Open prostatectomy
Likelihood of symptoms improving	10-15%	30-60%	44-65%	75-96%	75%	90%
Risk of immediate complications or side-effects	No	5-15%	5-10%	15-20%	10-15%	20-40%
Risk of incontinence	No	No	No	3%	Less than 1%	3-5%
Risk of impotence	No	No	3-5% (reversible)	5-10%	Less than 2%	10-20%
Risk of retrograde ejaculation	No	3-5%	No	60-80%	10-20%	70-90%

Association and published in October 1997 suggest that Efaprost – which costs £17.99 for a month's supply of 90 capsules – can help relieve symptoms of BPH in some cases.

A total of 106 men took three Efraprost capsules daily for three months. All were asked to complete a questionnaire at the beginning and end of the study period. Of the men who had not previously taken any medication, 73% reported an improvement in their symptoms.

The main advantage in trying an over-the-counter product rather than taking drugs, such as finasteride or alpha-blockers, which your doctor can prescribe, is that these products do not appear to produce side-effects. However, the Prostate Help Association warns that since the price of saw palmetto extract has rocketed, it is important to buy products from a reputable source and avoid cheap alternatives.

One of their newsletters says: "The saw palmetto capsule you buy cheaply via newspaper advertisements could be the leaves and stalks of the plant ground to powder and not the berry extract which contains the active ingredients. The capsule may be a good placebo but it will not be the herbal treatment. So be warned!"

case history:

"It started when I was living in America. I'd get up in the night to go to the toilet, then I'd stand there and nothing would happen. We didn't have medical cover, so I didn't do anything about it until we came back to Britain six months or so later. But I'm the kind of man who likes to get things sorted, so then I saw a GP pretty quickly.

"He gave me a DRE. I wasn't embarrassed – not when it was a question of my health. I could actually feel there was some kind of obstruction when he put his finger up.

"The next step was for me to see a consultant at the hospital. It took about eleven weeks for the appointment to come through. He gave me another DRE, and took samples of blood and urine. He confirmed I had an enlarged prostate and put me on the waiting list for an operation.

"In the meantime I had to go back to see the consultant at regular intervals. On one of the visits I had to drink a litre of water, wait an hour and then go for an ultrasound scan. By that time I was in agony and felt as if I would burst. But when I was allowed to go to the toilet my flow still wasn't good. The consultant said I had massive retention of urine.

"I had asked my GP if it could be cancer, and no one would rule it out, but I was reassured by knowing that even if it was, the clear-up rate was good if caught early. My GP also told me about doing autopsies on men of 90 who turned out to have prostate cancer which had never bothered them at all.

"The hospital sent me an information sheet about the prostatectomy operation which was comprehensive and answered questions I hadn't even thought to ask.

"I had the operation the day after I was admitted. When I came round from the anaesthetic they told me I was a 'bleeder' and they'd had to give me four pints of blood. The old boy in the bed next to me was out in two days, but I was still passing blood and debris and draining copious amounts of water to flush it through.

"Two days after the operation they took the catheter out. They warned me that some men had to have it put back in again, but my flow was fine although it now smarted quite a bit – and did for the next two weeks – and there was still blood in my urine.

"I was told that this was perfectly normal and, for me, the operation has been a complete success. I was relieved when they told me that a biopsy showed it wasn't a cancerous growth and I still have no problems with urination three years later.
Mr GB, aged 63, from Kent.

Information about BPH is available from:

Prostate Help Association
Langworth, Lincoln, LN3 5DF.
For initial information, send two first class stamps. A personal account of Thermex treatment is available, but a donation of £5 to the charity is requested.

Prostate Research Campaign UK
36, The Drive, Northwood, Middlesex HA6 1HP
Send a 9x7 inch sae for information and leaflets.

Information about Thermex treatment for BPH:
Direx Medical Systems
Mantra House, South Street, Keighley, W Yorks BD21 1SX
01535 691001

Information on Efaprost
Efamol Information Line 01483 570248

Information about fertility services including sperm banks:
Human Fertilisation and Embryology Authority
30 Artillery Lane, London E1 7LS 0171 377 5077

ISSUE
509 Aldridge Road, Great Barr, B44 8NA 0121 344 4414
Supplies information about infertility to members. Membership costs £30 for the first year, £20 pa thereafter.

NIAC, the National Infertility Awareness Campaign
37 Soho Square, London W1V 5DG 0171 439 3067

CHAPTER FIVE

....

prostate cancer: part I

For men in the UK, cancer of the prostate is the third most common cancer and the second biggest cause of cancer deaths. As a killer it is only beaten by lung cancer, and only lung cancer and skin cancer are more common among men. Although it is rare in men under 45 and generally occurs in those who have passed middle age, prostate cancer is responsible for some 9,500 deaths a year.

INCIDENCE

In the UK during 1991 (the most recent figures available) 273,130 new cases of cancer were registered, 135,040 of them in men. The 10 cancers that occur most commonly in men are shown below.

Number

28,420	**Lung**	21%
16,930	**Skin***	13%
15,550	**Prostate**	12%
9,260	**Bladder**	7%
9,220	**Colon**	7%
6.920	**Stomach**	5%
6,510	**Rectum**	5%
3,890	**NHL****	3%
3,540	**Oesophagus**	3%
3,410	**Pancreas**	3%
135,040	All malignant neoplasms***	100%

*Non-melanoma skin cancer
**Non Hodgkin's lymphoma
*** Excludes benign and in-situ neoplasms (tumours) and those of uncertain behaviour and unspecified nature
Source: Cancer Research Campaign

No one knows exactly what causes prostate cancer, but age, race and heredity are recognised risk factors and cancer of the prostate is becoming more common in the developed world. This may partly be due to the fact that it is diagnosed more accurately than it used to be, but there is evidence to suggest that a Western lifestyle – one where people tend to have a diet high in fat and low in vegetables – may also be partly to blame.

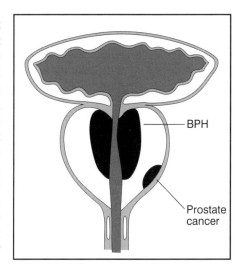

Incidence and mortality rates for prostate cancer vary widely throughout the world but reliable information in often difficult to obtain since, in many countries, data cannot be recorded or collected accurately. This means that for much of the world's population, researchers have to estimate incidence and mortality rates.

The Cancer Research Campaign has tried to collect as much international data as possible to give a general overview about the world burden of cancer. Prostate cancer was estimated to account for four per cent of new cancers worldwide in 1985. However, the distribution of cancer between the developed world and the developing countries is markedly different, with prostate cancer being much more common in the developed world.

The highest reported incidence rates are in black American men, with age-standardised rates running as high as 102 per 100,000 population – around 50% more than in the US white male population, although even these rates are higher than elsewhere in the world. Sweden and Norway also have high reported rates, as does Brazil.

At the other end of the scale, low rates are recorded in Asian countries: the figures from China are under 2 per 100,000. In Japan the rates are around 6 per 100,00 but these figures appear to be rising. Studies of Japanese who have settled in the US also show that migrants from low to high risk countries increase their risk within one generation.

This suggests that life-style is important, although genetics may also play a role, since American Japanese incidence rates do not generally become as high as white American rates.
In the UK, incidence rates vary, too. Incidence rates for Scotland, for instance, are higher than those for England and Wales.

Prostate cancer may also run in families. Evidence suggests that the risk is greater if the affected relative is young or if more than one relative is affected. Men whose families have an increased risk of breast cancer also appear to be at higher risk of prostate cancer. Research is now going on to try to determine the gene or genes which predispose a family to prostate cancer.

Other possible risk factors may include exposure to cadmium or radiation, and a man's sexual history (the age he first had sex and the number of sexual partners he has had). Although some studies have pointed to a link between vasectomy and prostate cancer, doubts have since been cast on this contention, and the current view is that there is little evidence of a definite link.

what is prostate cancer?
The simple answer is that it is a malignant cancer which occurs in the prostate because of a change in the way cells grow and divide.

The organs and tissues of the body are made up of minute building blocks called cells. Although cells in different parts of the body look and function differently, most repair and reproduce themselves in the same way. Normally, cells divide in an orderly and controlled manner but if this process gets out of control, the cells continue to divide, developing into a tumour. Tumours can be benign or malignant.

In a benign tumour, the cells do not spread to other parts of the body and are therefore not cancerous. If a benign tumour grows too large, however, it may still cause problems by pressing on surrounding organs.

In a malignant tumour, the cancer cells have the ability to spread beyond the original, primary site. If left untreated they may invade and destroy surrounding tissue. Sometimes cells break away from the original cancer, spreading to other organs in the body via the bloodstream or lymphatic system. When they reach a new site they may go on dividing and growing to form a new tumour, which is then referred to as a secondary or metastasis. In order to determine whether a tumour is benign or malignant, a sample of its cells are examined under a microscope. This is known as a biopsy.

Prostate cancer seems to arise from an imbalance of certain chemicals which control prostate cell growth. There may also be damage to the genetic material (DNA) in the prostate cells, causing the uncontrolled growth of the cells.

Like BPH, prostate cancer becomes increasingly common with advancing age: nearly three-quarters of men in their 80s will have small lesions of prostate cancer, although only a few of these will eventually develop symptoms. Cancer of the prostate can exist with BPH and may be detected when men undergo a transurethral prostatectomy (TURP) for this condition. Prostate cancer is also becoming increasingly common in younger men.

One of the difficulties facing doctors, who have to make decisions about whether to screen for prostate cancer, and what to do if they find it, is that we know that prostate cancer does not usually cause symptoms until it is well advanced, yet can be cured if caught early.

The doctors' dilemma is that there is no sure-fire way of knowing which lesions will progress slowly and which will prove to be aggressive. This is sometimes referred to as sorting out the grumblers from the growlers, or the tigers from the pussycats.

the PSA test and the screening debate

Since prostate cancer is one of the commonest cancers men suffer from, parallels are often drawn between it and breast cancer in women. Women in Britain are now invited to attend regular screening for breast cancer, courtesy of the NHS, once they reach the age of 50. In recent years there has been a growing public pressure for a similar programme to be set up to screen for prostate cancer in older men.

The most sensitive screening tests for prostate cancer are based on levels of prostate specific antigen – PSA. However, there is still a great deal of debate as to whether or not it is worth introducing these tests as part of a nationwide screening programme for prostate cancer.

As long ago as the 1970s, a group of scientists identified PSA, a protein that the prostate, and only the prostate, releases into the blood. They discovered that a man's PSA level was rather like a thermometer – a sudden rise could indicate he had a problem with his prostate.

Raised PSA levels may point to an infection or prostate enlargement (BPH). But because they may also indicate prostate cancer, the development of the PSA test seemed a great step forward. Since prostate cancer can be symptomless in the early stages, many men were unaware they had it until the disease progressed, perhaps spreading to the lymph nodes or bones. At last, it looked as if doctors would be able to detect prostate cancer long before this happened.

The test wasn't complicated, uncomfortable or embarrassing. All the patient had to do was give a sample of blood. If PSA levels were raised or rising, the next step would be a biopsy. If this indicated cancer, a radical prostatectomy could be performed, removing the prostate, hopefully before the cancer had had a chance to spread elsewhere. Of course, surgery had its own risks including the possibility of a man being left impotent, incontinent, or both. Even so, doctors argued, being able to detect prostate cancer quickly would save the lives of thousands of men every year.

Today, in the United States, PSA tests for older men are commonplace. It is not unknown for anxious Americans to check their levels monthly, like the balance in their bank account. The American Cancer Society and American Urological Association recommend annual PSA tests for men over 50 and for high risk men – those with a close family history of prostate cancer, for instance.

Yet in Britain, the NHS Centre for Reviews and Dissemination at the University of York says routine screening of men to detect prostate cancer should be discouraged, irrespective of family history. Even in America, there are those – including one of the scientists who discovered PSA – who believe that things have got out of hand.

Why? It's true that since the introduction of the PSA test in America, the number of prostate cancers detected has been rising. There, this increase in diagnosis has been accompanied by an increase in treatment. However, both urologists and oncologists differ greatly in their views as to whether this is, in itself, a good thing.

Not all prostate cancers grow aggressively. Many men die with prostate cancer rather than as a result of it. The difficulty for doctors, once cancer has been detected in the prostate, is deciding whether it is a "pussy cat" or a "tiger". In parts of Europe and in the United Kingdom, many specialists are in favour of "watchful waiting", particularly where the cancer is localised and man is getting on in years. Yet in the United States there has been an increasing tendency to use radical prostatectomy in men over 70 and some American commentators have questioned the wisdom of this, given the possible complications.

In the UK, Joan Austoker, director of the Cancer Research Campaign Primary Care Education Research Group, examined the issues surrounding screening for prostate cancer. In her view, the most cost effective approach to early detection would seem to be a combination of digital rectal examination (DRE) and PSA tests, followed by transrectal ultrasound if necessary. In a paper published in the *British Medical Journal* in 1994, she wrote: "Even with this combined approach, however . . . . many cancers will be missed, false positive results will be high and many cancers will be diagnosed that would otherwise have remained latent. As the specificity of the three tests is comparatively poor, a fairly high proportion of screened subjects with suspicious results in one or more of these tests will need to undergo a prostatic biopsy without having the disease. This is a disturbing observation."

She summarised the problems in screening for prostatic cancer.

- Relatively unimportant cause of premature mortality - that is, few potential years of life saved
- No clear evidence that screening and treatment will reduce mortality from the disease
- Enormous scope for overdiagnosis (detection of clinically insignificant disease)
- Absence of an acceptable and valid test to determine accurately which cancers will remain latent and which will progress
- Low specificity, sensitivity and positive predictive value of existing tests
- Uncertainty about the appropriate treatment for early disease
- Side effects of treatment for cancer detected on screening
- Psychological consequences for those found to have preclinical disease; in most cases the disease would not have progressed
- Financial costs of screening
- The ethics of screening for the disease – more harm may be caused than benefit.

Three years later, in the February 1997 issue of *Effectiveness Matters*, the NHS Centre for Reviews and Dissemination took the same line. The report said: "Unlike breast cancer screening, which has been shown to reduce mortality, prostate cancer screening has not yet been evaluated and there are several reasons why it may be less effective.

"Many men with prostate cancer never experience any ill-effects because some tumours are slow growing and not aggressive. The most sensitive screening tests for prostate cancer are based on levels of PSA. However, the PSA test and follow up biopsies cannot predict reliably whether a man has a cancer that will progress to cause ill health or death.

"There have been no reliable evaluations of the effect of treatments for early prostate cancer on mortality. Active treatments can result in major complications such as incontinence and impotence. There is no evidence on the number of deaths (if any) which could be averted by screening asymptomatic men. Screening may lead to physical and psychological harm resulting from testing, biopsy and treatment. It is not known whether screening for prostate cancer does more harm than good."

The Centre has produced a leaflet for men considering or asking for PSA tests. Not surprisingly, its overall tone is less than encouraging. However, this stance has been hotly challenged by some leading urologists and prostate charity campaigners.

The Prostate Research Campaign UK says that the Centre's conclusions – that men should not be offered the chance of early detection and treatment until such procedures are proven beyond doubt – are both negative and unhelpful. They argue that since the death rates from prostate cancer in England and Wales have almost doubled in the past 25 years, and are projected to double again in the next two decades, action must be taken now to avert this crisis.

In addition, they say that the reviews were based on studies which – in the words of the charity's founder Anthony Kilmister – are "already growing whiskers." They believe that current and future studies will tell quite a different story and point to the fact that data emerging in the US indicate for the first time that screening and active treatment policies have led to a 9% fall in mortality for prostate cancer.

"No one is suggesting that the PSA test is perfect," says Mr Kilmister. "But so far it's the best we've got. The fact that it is not perfect is no excuse for inaction. It's just the NHS finding reasons for doing nothing.

"It is nonsense for some people to claim that PSA testing promotes stress and anxiety and has no value. Based on that way of thinking, breast and cervical screening for women would also have no value. Any test – such as a driving test – creates stress and anxiety but driving tests are necessary if we are to keep crazy motorists from charging up the motorway.

"And this business of "more men die with prostate cancer than of it" – I suspect that more men die with vascular disease than of it, yet we still treat it.

"Too many negative attitudes surround the operation known as radical prostatectomy. American enthusiasms went too far, but British experts do not charge in like a bull in a china shop. They are much more cautious. Even so, the wisdom of the age has not caught up with the art of the possible.

"Every prostate cancer death begins with a very small tumour. While a prostate cancer is still contained there is a window of curability. There ought not to be any excuse NOT to treat prostate cancer. Instead there should be a crusade to catch it early."

Roger Kirby, consultant urologist at St George's Hospital, points out that PSA tests can be used not only to help diagnose the presence of prostate cancer, but to measure whether or not it is starting to spread. "The earlier cancer is diagnosed the more likely we can undertake curative therapy, if necessary, rather than merely palliative therapy."

He accepts the fact that there is no evidence currently available which proves screening for prostate cancer saves lives, but argues that the technology has not been in use long enough for this kind of evidence to come through.

"It's the doctor's dilemma: things are moving so fast that our ability to invent new technologies is outrunning our ability to test how effective they are."

While calling for more trials to be carried out to examine all the issues involved, he believes there is already enough supporting evidence to suggest PSA testing is worthwhile.

Opponents of screening often argue that being told you have prostate cancer, particularly if this turns out to be slow growing and non-aggressive, leaves men living out their lives in fear. The suggestion seems to be that what you don't know, can't hurt you.

Mr Kilmister says that being denied screening can leave men living their lives with a blindfold on. Mr Kirby has a similar view. "With PSA screening some men will be reassured. And those who find out they have cancer will, at least, have the chance to be treated. Of course, if you believe that by allowing people to bury their heads in the sand is enough to keep them happy, fair enough.

"I feel that from the age of 50 onwards, if you have an annual PSA test it might well save you dying from prostate cancer. But by the time we can prove this, for many men it will be too late."

how easy is it to get the PSA test?
The simple answer is that it all depends on where you live, what opinions your doctors hold and how persistent you are. Different GPs, for example, would respond differently if a man aged 50 came to see them asking for a PSA test.

Dr B, from Nottingham says:
"I'd want to know why the patient was requesting the test, what the problem was. It might not have anything to do with prostate cancer, it could be a worry about his sex life or his potency. If he was asking for the test because he was worried about the risks of cancer, it would be important to deal with what that might mean in terms of treatment and the future. For some men, being told they have prostate cancer feels like a death sentence. So I'd make sure I explained that many older men die with, not from, prostate cancer. I'd explain that it has now been shown that the test is not as reliable as was once thought. You can get false positives and false negatives. If the patient still wanted the test to be done, I'd do it and I'd do a

DRE. If the levels were only slightly raised I probably wouldn't take any action if there weren't any other symptoms, other than suggesting he repeat the test a year later. If I had any doubt, I'd refer the patient to a urologist. Overall I would try to dissuade a patient from getting on the treadmill of annual PSA tests because I think that, rather than solving problems, they cause more worry.

Dr K from North London says:
"I'd want to find out why he was asking for the tests. If he had symptoms or a family history of prostate cancer, I'd do the test. If that wasn't the case I'd explain that screening itself is not very helpful. I'd say that some research has shown that one blood test when you don't have any signs or symptoms can be misleading or confusing. But if he still insisted he wanted the test done, I'd do it. You don't want to lay yourself open, just in case he goes off and has the test done somewhere else and he turns out to have cancer.

Dr I from North Yorks says:
"I'd explain that the PSA test is not totally reliable and a positive result may mean undergoing unpleasant investigation. I'd also say that even if early cancer is found, opinion is divided on how best to treat it or even if it is best left alone."

Dr M from Hertfordshire says:
"If his father or uncles had suffered from prostate cancer I could be persuaded to carry out a PSA test. Strength of family history can be important and in those circumstances I think it would be reasonable to screen on an annual basis after the age of 50."

If your GP is unwilling to carry out a PSA test there are other places you can try, if you are prepared to pay:
Marie Stopes clinics in London, Manchester and Leeds offer well man screening. A Well Man Plus screen includes a PSA test. The price in 1997 was £75.

Depending on your age and personal health risks a PSA test is available as part of the BUPA Full Health Monitor package. In 1997 this assessment cost £340 or £290 for BUPA members. BUPA has 31 centres where health checks are carried out. Clearly, paying for a full health check simply to get a PSA test is an expensive way of going about things, and it should be possible to find a doctor who will do the test privately for a price between £20 and £30.

If you check the Yellow Pages, you may find some doctors advertising private medicals and health screening services. The Independent Healthcare Association may be able to give some leads if you have to search for a clinic or hospital in your locality willing to offer a PSA test. The IHA won't be able to tell you which tests or screens are done in different places, but they will be able to tell you which independent healthcare providers are on their records as offering screening services. It will then be up to you to call them individually to find out if they offer what you want, and what this would cost. They prefer phone calls to letters and can be contacted on 0171 430 0537.

Marie Stopes Well Man Screening
London: 108 Whitfield Street, London W1P 6BE (0171 388 0662)
Manchester: St John's Street Chambers, 2 St John's Street, Manchester M3 4DB (0161 832 4260
Leeds: 10 Queen's Square, Leeds LS2 8AJ (0113 2440685)

BUPA
BUPA House, 15-19 Bloomsbury Way, London WC1A 2BA
Health Monitor is available at all BUPA Screening Centres. For more information call 0800 616029.

CHAPTER SIX
....

prostate cancer: part II

Unlike BPH, prostate cancer usually develops in the outer part of the prostate gland. Doctors usually talk about the prostate in terms of three zones : the peripheral zone, the central zone and the transition zone. Studies have shown that 70% of prostate cancers arise in the peripheral zone, 15-20% in the central zone and 10-15% in the transition zone.

As a cancer enlarges, it may begin to invade the seminal vesicle (the gland where semen is stored). It may also start to press on the urethra, causing problems with urination.

Eventually, cells from the cancer may break away and spread to other parts of the body via the bloodstream or the lymphatic system. When the cells reach a new site they may start to form a new cancer, called a secondary or metastasis. The lymph nodes, the bones, as well as the lungs, are the sites most commonly affected by these secondary cancers.

what to watch out for:
Prostate cancer is often symptomless in the very early stages. If it starts to press on the urethra as it grows it may cause symptoms which are similar to those of BPH. These include:
● difficulty in passing urine
● passing urine more frequently than usual, especially at night
● pain on passing urine
● blood in the urine

If you experience any of the above symptoms it is important to have them checked out by a doctor, but at this stage it is worth remembering that most enlargements of the prostate are due to BPH, a benign condition, which can be treated.

Cancer of the prostate is often a slow growing cancer, particularly in older men and symptoms may not occur for many years. If the cancer does eventually spread to secondary sites, it may only be then that symptoms occur. These may include:
● weight loss
● pain in the bones of the pelvis, legs and especially the lower back

If you have developed lower back pain and are experiencing difficulties in passing urine, this may be a warning that you have prostate cancer. However, most cases of back pain are due to arthritis of the spine.

how do doctors tell if you have prostate cancer?
The first two tests which a GP will carry out will be a DRE and a blood test. Prostate cancer often causes a change in the gland which can be felt by the doctor when he puts his gloved finger inside the rectum. Normally the prostate should feel smooth or elastic. If it feels nodular, hard or woody, this may indicate cancer.

The sample of blood will be checked for a "marker" called PSA (prostate specific antigen). A high level can be a sign of cancer, although PSA levels may also be raised in men who have benign prostate conditions. PSA levels also rise with age. The upper limit of normal for PSA is 4.0 nanograms/millilitre. Levels only a little higher than this are often due to BPH. In general, the higher the level of PSA, the greater the risk of cancer. (Once a cancer has been treated, PSA levels fall. They are also checked throughout treatment as a way of seeing how the cancer is responding.)

If the tests suggest any abnormalities, your GP will refer you to hospital for further investigations. There, a biopsy can be carried out to confirm whether cancer is present or not.

An antibiotic is given to minimise the risk of infection, then several samples – tiny pieces of prostate tissue – are taken using a very fine needle which is inserted via the rectum. The tissue is then sent to a laboratory and examined under a microscope to check for cancer cells.

Ultrasound is often used to help the surgeon guide the biopsy needle. A finger-sized probe is put into the rectum. Sound waves are then passed through the prostate. These bounce back off the tissue and are converted into an image on a computer screen.

Having a biopsy may be uncomfortable but is not particularly painful, although a needle prick may be felt as each sample of tissue is removed. Afterwards, patients sometimes see some blood in their urine, semen or stools. Occasionally infection occurs, which can be treated with further antibiotics.

Cancer can come to light in a different way: prostate tissue removed from men suffering from BPH, who have been admitted to hospital for surgery to reduce the size of the prostate, is usually biopsied. Sometimes cancer is found.

what if cancer is detected?

In order to decide what course of treatment is most appropriate, doctors need to know what stage the cancer has reached and how far it has spread. A number of imaging techniques can be used to assist them. These include:

ultrasound

As described above, a finger sized probe is inserted into the rectum, using sound waves to produce a picture of the prostate on a computer screen.

x-ray

A chest X-ray and X-ray of the bones may be taken to see if there is any spread of cancer

isotope bone scan

Bone scans are so sensitive they can detect cancer cells before they show up on X-ray. They highlight abnormal blood flow in bone, which may be due to cancer which has spread from the prostate.A small dose of a mildly radioactive isotope is injected into a vein, usually in your arm. It takes two to three hours for the isotope to be taken up by the bones and you may be allowed to leave the outpatients department while this occurs. In any case, it is probably a good idea to take a book to read or some music to listen to while you wait.

Next, you have to lie on a table while a special scanning camera is passed over your body. As abnormal bone absorbs more of the isotope than normal bone, this shows up on the scan as highlighted patches. All of your skeleton will be scanned, with particular attention paid to your spine, pelvis and ribs.

MRI or CT scans
These give more detailed information about the prostate. They take several pictures from different angles. The information is fed into a computer which can then produce detailed images of the prostate and may show the extent of the cancer if it is present. The scans can also show if secondaries have formed in other tissues. The tests may make you feel a bit claustrophobic but they are not painful.

CT stands for computed tomography. You may be given an injection in your arm of a contrast agent. You may also be given a contrast agent to drink. This helps increase the detail of the pictures. The injection may make you feel hot all over for a few minutes.

You then lie on a table which is passed through a large hoop-shaped scanner while the X-rays are taken. This does not hurt. but you have to lie still for about 30-40 minutes.

MRI – magnetic resonance imaging – does not involve the use of X-rays, although the procedure is similar to CT scanning. In this case the scanner is a large, powerful magnet. During the test you have to lie very still on a table which is passed into a metal cylinder containing the magnet. The scan is noisy and may make you feel uncomfortable but you can usually take someone into the room with you to keep you company. As magnetism is involved, you cannot take anything metal into the scanning tunnel and so this procedure is not suitable for people with pacemakers, hip replacements or other implants containing metal.

treatment:

If you have prostate cancer your treatment will depend on a number of factors, including your age, your general health, and the type, size and spread of the cancer. These days a combination of treatments may be used to get the best results.

Doctors often talk about staging cancer, which means using strict measures to determine the extent of cancer in an individual. This helps them decide on the best treatment. *(see page 110)*

The cancer is described in terms of how large the main tumour is, the degree to which it has invaded surrounding tissue and the extent to which it has spread to lymph glands or other areas of the body. You may be told your cancer is localised i.e., confined to the prostate. In many cases immediate treatment will not be thought necessary since the cancer may never progress fast enough to cause any problems. Alternatively you may be offered radiotherapy or surgery.

If you are told your cancer is locally advanced, that means it has spread quite widely into surrounding tissue but has not reached more distant parts of the body. You may be offered hormonal therapy and/or radiotherapy.

An advanced cancer is one which has spread to the bones or elsewhere in the body. Drugs can be given to deprive the cancer cells of the male hormones they need to grow and spread. This usually brings about a period of remission. Unfortunately, most advanced prostate cancers begin to grow again after a while. This relapse is known as hormone escape.

You may meet or know other men with prostate cancer, and discover that their treatment is different from yours. This may be because their illness takes a different form and they therefore have different needs. It may be that their doctor takes a different view about the appropriate treatment.

Don't be afraid to ask your doctor why he is recommending a

particular treatment and whether there is an alternative. Some people find it helps to have a second medical opinion to help them decide what is best to do. Most doctors understand this and will refer you to another specialist for this if you feel it would be helpful.

Treatment for prostate cancer can cause unpleasant long-term side effects, including impotence and urinary incontinence. It is also likely to cause infertility. Often doctors cannot predict accurately who will be affected and who won't, which is why it is important to ask about the risks associated with different kinds of treatment and to discuss everything fully with your specialist and your family.

treatment for localised prostate cancer

watchful waiting:

If the cancer is confined to the prostate it is unlikely to cause problems for five years or more. This means that in older men, or men with other illnesses which limit life expectancy, watchful waiting may be the best option, given that treatment for prostate cancer inevitably has side effects. Even so, regular examinations and measurements of PSA levels should be carried out, so that treatment can be considered if the cancer appears to be progressing. If your doctor recommends watchful waiting it is important to let him know at once if you detect any changes in your condition, rather than waiting for your next appointment.

There are some things you can do which may help fight off the cancer during this watchful waiting time.

● Watch your diet. Eating less animal fat and more fresh fruit, vegetables and fish may help slow down the growth of the cancer and will be good for your general health.
● Stop smoking. Smoking doesn't cause prostate cancer but may cause it to spread more quickly.
● Reduce stress. Learn to relax if you can. Try relaxation tapes. Take up a new hobby. Join a support group. Talk to your doctor about how you feel about watchful waiting. Some people find the idea of not having treatment stressful in itself. You may feel reassured when

your doctor explains how close an eye will be kept on you and what the treatment options may be.

● Your specialist may suggest a course of antibiotics. In a few cases infection may speed up the development of prostate cancer.

radiotherapy:

This is a common treatment for localised cancer. The prostate is bombarded with carefully calculated doses of radiation, similar to X-rays, to kill cancer cells while doing as little harm as possible to normal cells.

Radiotherapy itself is not painful but it can cause side effects such as diarrhoea, bleeding and discomfort in the rectum, painful or frequent urination, or occasionally blood in the urine. About one man in fifty subsequently suffers incontinence. Impotence is also a common side effect – the figures suggest that between 25% and 50% of patients cannot achieve an erection following treatment.

Treatment may not always inactivate all the cancer cells in the prostate, so the disease may recur. According to the Prostate Research Campaign UK, in some centres up to 60% of men have survived for 15 years after treatment, while in others results have been more disappointing. A rise in PSA levels following radiotherapy suggests other treatment is necessary. However, even if radiotherapy fails to kill off all the cancer cells it may slow the spread to other areas of the body.

If you are given radiotherapy, a treatment plan will be drawn up. It often means attending a hospital radiotherapy department as an out-patient from Monday to Friday, with a rest at the weekend, for a number of weeks.

The radiographer will draw marks on your skin to show where the rays have to be directed. These should only be washed off after your course of treatment is over.

Before each session the radiographer will get you in the right position on the couch. You then have to lie still for a few minutes while the treatment is given. Although you will be alone for this, you will be able to talk to the radiographer who will be watching from an adjoining room.

Radiotherapy can make you feel very tired, especially if you are having to get up several times in the night. It's important to try and get as much rest as you can during treatment. It is also important to drink plenty of fluids and eat a healthy diet. If you do not have much of an appetite, try high calorie drink supplements which are available at most chemists. If diarrhoea is a problem, mention this to your doctor as it can be usually be treated with drugs. Avoid high fibre foods.

Occasionally cancer of the prostate is treated by internal radiotherapy. Small radioactive beads are inserted into the tumour under a general anaesthetic. The beads release radiation slowly over a period of time until they become inactive. There is no risk of the radiation affecting other people.

Radiotherapy is also given to patients with advanced cancer where tumours have spread to the bones. This can be an effective way of helping to reduce pain.

trans-urethral resection
If part of the tumour in your prostate is blocking the urethra and causing urinary difficulties you may be given an operation known as trans-urethral resection. This is generally done under general anaesthetic, although an epidural (spinal anaesthetic) may be used instead. A tube is passed via the penis, through the urethra, and an instrument attached to the inside of the tube is used to cut away the blockage. A catheter will be inserted so that your urine can be drained off into a bag. This is usually removed after 36 to 48 hours. Most men can go home after three or four days.

radical prostatectomy
If the cancer is confined to the prostate, then surgically removing the entire gland offers the best prospects of a cure. Figures cited by the Prostate Research Campaign UK suggest that 80 per cent of

patients are still alive 10 years after the operation and 60 per cent after 15 years.

However, this is a complex operation which is carried out less often in the UK than in the US and is usually only considered for younger men with high grade tumours that have not spread beyond the prostate. It carries a high risk of impotence and a lesser one of incontinence, although improvements in techniques (in particular the development of what doctors call nerve sparing prostatectomy) mean that these complications are less common than they used to be. Even so, about 2% of men will be left incontinent and from 50% to 70% impotent.

Many doctors feel that radical prostatectomy is most suitable for younger men with a life expectancy of more than 10 years: there is some debate as to whether it can ever be justified in older men.

Some doctors remove the lymph nodes in the pelvis by key-hole surgery some weeks before a radical prostatectomy is scheduled, so that they can be examined to see whether the cancer has already spread beyond the prostate itself. Sometimes these nodes are removed for examination once the patient has been opened up for prostate surgery. In either case, if there is evidence that the cancer has already progressed outside the prostate, the surgeon may decide not to proceed with a radical prostatectomy after all.

A radical prostatectomy normally takes two to four hours. A vertical incision is made in the abdominal wall between your navel and your pubis, but the surgeon does not cut through the membrane which contains your abdominal organs. The entire prostate gland and seminal vesicles are removed. A catheter is inserted via the penis into the bladder. The urethra is rejoined to the bladder over the catheter which acts as a splint and is left in place for about two weeks.

When you come round you will probably have a drain in your stomach which will be removed after a couple of days when the wound is leaking less blood and fluid. You may be given pain relief intravenously or by patient-controlled analgesia.

At first you will probably have an intravenous drip in your arm, to replace the fluid lost during the operation. Unless there are contra-indications, you may have heparin injections to reduce the risk of blood clots, until you are mobile.

When you leave hospital – probably within five to seven days – the urinary catheter may still be in place. This won't be removed until everything has healed up.

As this is major surgery you will need six to eight weeks to convalesce and you may feel weak and tired for several months.

Follow-up appointments will be necessary, although the intervals between them will depend on the normal practice of your consultant. He will want to check your PSA levels. These should fall after surgery and stay low; if the levels rise this usually means cancer is still present or has recurred and may need further treatment.

treatment for locally advanced prostate cancer
When cancer has spread beyond the prostate doctors know that it is important to deprive the cancer cells of androgens, the male hormones necessary for them to grow and spread. This can be done in a number of ways.

The aim is to stop the normal chain of events which starts when the hypothalamus in the brain releases LHRH (luteinising hormone releasing hormone).This stimulates the pituitary gland to produce another hormone, LH (luteinising hormone). LH then stimulates the testes to produce the male hormone testosterone.

But by reducing the amount of testosterone being produced it is possible to slow down the growth of a tumour, or shrink it, and symptoms often disappear.

orchidectomy
One way of interrupting the chain and reducing the production of testosterone is to surgically remove the testes – castration. Doctors call this a bilateral orchidectomy and it can be carried out in a matter

of minutes through a scrotal incision under local, regional or light general anaesthetic. However, most patients are likely to have deep concerns about the cosmetic and psychological impact of having their testes removed and, as a result, many prefer a medical rather than a surgical approach.

drug treatments

Another way of interrupting the chain which leads to the production of testosterone is by using drugs. Two types are used: sometimes on their own, increasingly together.

The first type may be referred to as pituitary downregulators, or, more likely, as LHRH or GnRH analogues or agonists. LHRH stands for luteinizing hormone-releasing hormone. GnRH stands for gonadotrophin releasing hormone. They include leuprolide (Prostap), buserelin (Suprefact) and goserelin acetate (Zoladex).

They are generally given by injection under the skin and you can have this done by your GP or community nurse.

The second type are the antiandrogens which come in tablet form. Even after treatment with LHRH analogues (or orchidectomy for that matter) some male hormones will still be produced. The action of these hormones can be blocked by antiandrogens, which include cyproterone acetate, flutamide and bicalutamide.

Antiandrogens counter "tumour flare": when patients start taking LHRH analogues they may experience a temporary surge of LH production which results in testosterone levels rising. This in turn may temporarily stimulate tumour growth. That is why your doctor should prescribe antiandrogens during the early weeks of treatment at least.

However, some studies suggest that treatment which continues to use a combination of both LHRH analogues and antiandrogens is more effective and produces a longer remission in this kind of cancer than treatment with LHRH analogues alone. This type of treatment is called total (or maximum) androgen blockade.

Treating prostate cancer with drugs is not a cure, but it may bring about a remission as well as shrinking the cancer. There is some evidence that tumours treated this way may be more susceptible to follow-up radiation or surgery.

However, these drugs can produce unpleasant side-effects such as impotence and hot flushes. The non-steroidal antiandrogen, flutamide, does not usually affect libido or potency when used alone. It may not be suitable for you, but you might wish to discuss this option with your doctor.

treatment for advanced cancer (metastatic disease)

In roughly four out of 10 cases, prostate cancer is only found when it has spread beyond the prostate to the bones or other organs. Drug treatment with LHRH analogues can be effective as prostate cancer secondaries almost always shrink if they are deprived of male hormones. Unfortunately, however, these tumours usually begin to grow again after a period of time. Doctors call this hormone escape.

Researchers hope that they will be able to develop gene therapy strategies to make hormone resistant cells sensitive to treatment again, but at present treatment for patients who have reached this point is aimed mainly at controlling the symptoms. Help may be available from palliative care teams, made up of doctors and nurses trained to look after people with advanced cancers. When prostate cancer spreads to the bones it can be extremely painful.

Radiotherapy – given to the affected bone or area – can help relieve pain. It may be given as a single treatment or a series of smaller treatments. Relief may be felt within a couple of days, although for some patients it may take three or four weeks to feel an improvement.

In some areas, men who have secondary tumours in their bones are offered treatment with strontium 90, a radioactive isotope which is given intravenously and taken up by the affected bones. Most men notice some improvement within a few weeks although occasionally the pain gets worse before it gets better.

Research is going on in a number of areas which hold out some promise for the future. Growth factor inhibitors and anti-tumour vaccines are being tested. This experimental work at least offers the hope that scientists will develop new treatments which may, one day, extend periods of remission or even find a cure for prostate cancer.

if you have cancer

If you are told you have prostate cancer your initial reaction to the diagnosis may very well be one of shock or disbelief. You may find it difficult to take in very much information at a time – and, in this, you won't be alone. Many patients with cancer find at first they have to keep asking the same questions over and again. This is a very common reaction to shock, yet the kind of numbness shock produces is a protection, a way of being able to function at all in a stressful situation.

Cancer patients often go through the same range of emotions people experience when they suffer a bereavement. At first they feel shocked and numb. Later they may feel very depressed. Their mood may swing from sadness to anger to fear. It is important to hold on to the fact that there isn't a right or a wrong way to feel. All these feelings are perfectly normal.

Admittedly, acknowledging your feelings may be difficult. The situation is often complicated by the fact that family and friends will be going through a similar range of emotions. You may feel unable to share your feelings, even with those closest to you, because you feel you have to put on a brave face.

Support groups can be useful in a number of ways. People with cancer often say that only those in the same situation can really understand how they feel and talking to an anonymous voice on the end of a telephone may be easier than talking face to face with your nearest or dearest. However, you may have to try a number of different organisations before you find one which suits you.

Hopefully, there will come a time when you will be able to acknowledge your feelings, accept the reality of the situation and move on. People often say that learning they had cancer made them rethink and redirect their lives: no-one ever wants to have cancer, but for many, it can almost be a gift in disguise. Having cancer can help people become aware of what really matters to them.

Admittedly, some men cope best at first by ignoring the news and carrying on with their lives as though nothing had happened. You may be one of them. However, after the initial shock, many men want to take a more adversarial approach, focusing on cancer as the enemy, keen to find out in depth what is known and what can be done.

There are a number of charities and support groups who can provide information, Some have specialist nurses to answer specific questions. Some have libraries and resource centres for cancer patients and their families.

You may have specific questions you want answered, specific worries which keep you awake at night. It often helps to write down a list of questions which you can take with you when you see your doctor. You may want to know how long you have got, how much pain you can expect. As a rule of thumb, it is best not to ask a question unless you want to hear the answer. And don't be surprised if your doctor doesn't give a clear answer. It does not mean he is hiding anything from you. Doctors are often surprised by patients they have given a poor prognosis to, so they tend to be cautious.

If you are depressed, don't close your eyes to the idea of getting medical help. Your GP can prescribe anti-depressants which can help. They need time to work: you will probably have to take a full dose for at least six weeks at which point your doctor will probably reduce the dose, and want you to continue for four to six months.

Research shows that the treatment is more effective and that depression is less likely to occur if a longer course is taken. Anti-depressants can cause side-effects including stomach upsets, dry mouth and lassitude, but if you experience any problems you should tell your doctor, and the dosage can be changed. Unlike tranquillisers, anti-depressants cannot cause dependency.

What else can you do to help yourself? Among all the others emotions, cancer patients often say they feel guilty. It's a natural tendency to blame oneself or others for what has happened and there is something in human nature which makes us feel a bit better if we know why things turned out the way they did. The trouble is, doctors rarely have an answer and it is better if you can come to accept that life isn't fair and this is just one of those things.

Psychotherapists and counsellors often use a technique called cognitive therapy, which aims to help people turn negative thoughts into positive ones. This can help you feel happier and more in control. You can find books about these techniques in bookshops and libraries, or you might like to see a therapist. Counselling gives you the chance to explore your feelings and experiences in an environment which is supportive and confidential.

Many people also find relaxation techniques helpful. Again, there are a number of reputable tapes and books available.

Another avenue you might wish to explore is complementary therapy. In general, it is wise to think of complementary medicine as being what it says, something you have alongside, rather than instead of, conventional medical care.

Complementary therapists usually take a holistic approach, which means you are seen as a whole person, with body, mind and spirit inter-relating and contributing to your state of health. Although some of the complementary therapies are available on the NHS, not all doctors accept them as being useful. On the other hand, many cancer patients say complementary therapies have been beneficial.

If you are interested, try to find a reliable practitioner. See if there is an organisation which sets standards and if they have a list of qualified members. Make sure you ask about costs before you embark on a course of treatment and try to find someone who has worked with people with cancer. Don't hesitate to ask for credentials and references and don't believe anyone who tells you there are miracle cures. If you decide to start using complementary therapy, it is sensible to tell your doctor. He will probably be supportive, but if not, you could ask if there is any valid medical reason for you not to go ahead.

case history

"I'd noticed I was having to go to lavatory more often than I used to, but I thought that was something that happens to all of us men and probably meant I had an enlarged prostate. So when my daughter – a GP – suggested I went for a PSA test I didn't rush off for one at once. It was only when my wife, who was also a GP, mentioned it again that I decided to get one done.

"She was horrifed when the reading came back high and, after having a word with a local urologist, suggested I had another one. That was high, too. So off I went to the urologist for a DRE. He found a tumour straight away and told me there was a good chance it was cancer. He had to do a biopsy. I felt shattered. I'd never felt fitter, yet here he was saying I might have cancer. I know now, of course, that fitness isn't the same as health. I had a rectal biopsy. I could hear the instrument they used going off like a starting pistol but it was uncomfortable rather than painful. Afterwards I had blood in my urine for a few days and that was frightening, although they told me it was normal.

"When the results came back there were some aspects which were reassuring. There was one tumour confined to the gland and it was a low grade cancer. But it was still cancer. The question was, what should I do now? Three months of heart searching and fact finding uncovered a minefield. But I felt sure there was no question of watchful waiting because of my age: I was still only 56. That left either surgery or radiotherapy.

"I went through the pros and cons, and the risk of complications in both cases seemed finely balanced. I still couldn't make up my mind. I saw two of the top men in the field – a urologist, who was also a surgeon, and a radiologist. The urologist gave me confidence. He said that if the operation was done by the right person, complications were less likely, so I decided to go ahead with surgery.

"After my radical prostatectomy I was very groggy for the first couple of days but well enough to go home on day nine. The catheter stayed in for 18 days and then I had to start to learn to control my bladder again. For a week I wore a pair of waterproof pants, but that was for self confidence more than anything else. I had no incontinence and potency returned over the next 18 months as the nerves repaired themselves.

"My surgeon said there was a 75% chance he'd got all the cancer, but it was impossible to be sure. My PSA level went right down, but was regularly monitored. Two years went by: then it started to rise again. Scans showed a small tumour had recurred in the area where the prostete used to be. I decided to hit it on the head once and for all.

"This time I took drugs for three months. The tumour shrank so much it could no longer be seen on a scan. Then I went ahead with radiotherapy. It lasted for six weeks, every day except weekends. Towards the end of the course I felt tired but, overall, it was not a big deal. My potency was affected but my consultant suggested Caverject. Luckily my wife was used to giving injections, so she injected me.

"When I first found out I had prostate cancer my reaction was: how could this happen to me? Then I decided things could have been worse: it wasn't a serious cancer, it could be dealt with - the question was, how? Now I've done surgery, I've done radiotherapy. If that doesn't work, it will be on to drugs. When you have cancer you can never entirely forget about it. Never a day goes by when you don't wonder if it's going to come back or spread and you're going to die.

"But I think I've been lucky. My cancer was caught early. If I hadn't gone for a PSA test, I'd sitting here with cancer spread now. Already my quality of life would be deteriorating. As it is, I've just been trekking in Nepal.
Mr B B, aged 60, from Windsor, Berks.

for more information or support

Action Cancer
1 Marlborough Park, Belfast BT9 6HQ
(01232 661081)
Information, advice and evening clinics for men concerned about prostate cancer. Cancer information centre and counselling service.

BACUP
3 Bath Place, Rivington Street, London EC2A 3JR
Cancer Information Service (0171 613 2121)
Freephone for callers outside London (0800 181199)
Cancer Counselling service 0171 696 9000 (London)
BACUP Scotland Cancer Counselling Service 0141 553 1553 (Glasgow)
Provides information about all aspects of cancer as well as emotional support for cancer patients, their families and friends. The Cancer Information Service is staffed by a team of specially trained nurses and supported by a panel of medical specialists. A wide range of booklets available. For publications information call 0171 696 9003.

British Association for Counselling
1 Regent Place, Rugby, CV21 2PJ
Information Line (01788 578328)
Can provide a list of trained counsellors and a publications sheet. Please send an sae with enquiries.

Bristol Cancer Help Centre
Grove House, Cornwallis Grove, Clifton, Bristol BS8 4PG
(0117 980 9500); Helpline (0117 980 9505)
Weekly holistic courses for cancer patients and their supporters which include counselling, relaxation, visualisation, meditation, art therapy, healing, dietary advice and vitamin supplements. The Bristol centre will provide a list of their own affiliated groups on request. A full list is also published in their news magazine Turning Point.

Cancer Care Society
Jane Scarth House, 39 The Hundred, Romsey, Hants SO51 8GE
(01794 830374)
Gives social and emotional support for people with cancer, their families and friends, through a national network of branches. Telephone and personal counselling by trained counsellors. Telephone link service for people with cancer to be put in touch with one another.

Chai – Lifeline Cancer Support and Centre for Help
Norwood House, Harmony Way, off Victoria Road, London NW4 2BZ
Helpline 0181 202 4567
Offers emotional support to Jewish cancer patients, their families and friends. One-to-one support by phone, at home, in hospital or hospice. Weekly support group and monthly coffee mornings. Complementary therapies offered. Resource library and medical lectures.

Cancerlink
11-21 Northdown Street, London N1 9BN
Cancerlink in Scotland
9 Castle Terrace, Edinburgh EH1 2DP
Freephone Cancer Information Helpline 0800 132905
Freephone Asian Cancer Information Helpline in Hindi, Bengali and English 0800 590415
Textphone available for deaf and hard of hearing people.
Booklets, audio tapes, leaflets and factsheets available. Cancerlink aims to promote self help and acts as a resource for around 500 support groups in the UK. They are developing networks of individual supporters.

Cancer Research Campaign
10 Cambridge Terrace, London NW1 4JL (0171 224 1333)
Can supply information about prostate cancer.

Gayscan
50 Avenue Road, London N12 8PY (0181 446 3896)
A national group offering confidential mutual support and help to

gay men living with cancer, their partners and carers. Runs a Telenet person-to-person telephone network. Send large sae for more information.

Hospice Information Service
St Christopher's Hospice, 51-59 Lawrie Park Road, Sydenham, London SE26 6DZ (0181 778 9252)
Publishes a directory of hospice and palliative care services giving details of hospices, home care and hospital support teams in the UK and the Republic of Ireland. For a copy, send a large sae with three 2nd class stamps.Telephone enquiries welcomed.

Institute for Complementary Medicine
PO Box 194, London SE16 1QZ (0171 237 5165)
Can supply names of practitioners in most kinds of complementary medicines. Also has contact with support groups. Send sae and three loose 1st class stamps, stating areas of interest.

Macmillan Cancer Relief
Anchor House, 15-19 Britten Street, London SW3 3TZ
(0171 351 7811)
Provides specialist advice and support through Macmillan nurses and doctors, and financial grants for people with cancer and their families.

Marie Curie Cancer Care
28 Belgrave Square, London SW1X 8QC (0171 235 3325)
Hands-on nursing care during the day and overnight in patients homes through the Marie Curie nursing service, free of charge to cancer patients. Also runs eleven Marie Curie Centres.

National Cancer Alliance
PO Box 579, Oxford, OX4 1LB (01865 793566)
Aims to bring cancer patients, health professionals, their relatives and friends together to work to improve cancer services and treatments throughout the UK. Publishes a Directory of Cancer Specialists to help cancer patients and their GPs identify who to contact in their area about cancer services and treatment.

Prostate Cancer Charity
Du Cane Road, London W12 0NN (0181 383 8124)
Raises money to fund research into prostate cancer. Also offers an information and support service. Telephone helpline open Thursday and Friday mornings: 0181 383 1948. Can provide a range of literature offering an overview of prostate cancer and common treatments available. Also has an internet home page: http://www.prostate-cancer.org.uk.

Prostate Research Campaign UK
36 The Drive, Northwood, Middlesex HA6 1HP (01923 824 278)
Registered charity formed to increase awareness of prostate disorders and to sponsor research into them. Information available includes Prostate Brief No 4 on prostate cancer.

PSA London (the London Prostate Cancer Support Association)
50 Avenue Road, London N12 8PY
Aims to encourage and assist the setting up of local support groups for men with prostate cancer. Networking to exchange information. Regular meetings in the City of London. Contact Angus: 0181 446 3896 10am-8pm; Mark 01634 570309 10am-8pm; Ray 0181 883 9571 5pm-11pm.

Sue Ryder Foundation
Cavendish, Sudbury, Suffolk, CO10 8AY (01787 280252)
Nine Sue Ryder Homes in England specialise in cancer care. Visiting nurses care for patients in their own homes. Advice, bereavement counselling and respite care.

Tak Tent Cancer Support
Block C20, Western Court, 100 University Place, Glasgow G12 6SQ (0141 211 1930)
Information, support, education and care for cancer patients, families and friends. Network of support groups across Scotland, meeting monthly in the evening.

Tenovus Cancer Information Centre
College Buildings, Courtenay Road, Splott, Cardiff CF1 1SA
Helpline 0800 526 527
Information and support on all aspects of cancer. Helpline staffed by experienced cancer trained nurses, counsellors and social workers. Drop-in Centre. Free patient literature.

Ulster Cancer Foundation
40-42 Eglantine Avenue, Belfast BT9 6DX
Helpline 01232 663439 9.30 -12.30 weekday mornings and Wed 2-4pm.
Telephone helpline and call-in service. Information on all aspects of cancer.

Suggested Further Reading
Cancerlink booklets: These include:
Men and Cancer
Body image, sexuality and cancer
Cancer and employment
Close relationships and cancer
Available from Cancerlink, 11-21 Northdown Street, London N1 9BN

Life After Cancer by Ann Kent, £8.99 Ward Lock. Written for people who have been treated for cancer.

Prostate Cancer by Philip Dunn, Secretary of the Prostate Help Association, £7.99 mail order from the PHA, Langworth, Lincoln LN3 5DF
The Cancer Guide, free BBC/Macmillan Cancer Relief booklet, PO Box 7, London W5 2GQ.

Understanding Cancer of the Prostate, free from BACUP, 3 Bath Place, Rivington Street, London EC2A 3JR

CHAPTER SEVEN
....

incontinence and impotence

Unfortunately, certain treatments for prostate problems carry the risk of complications which can have a significant impact on the quality of life: incontinence and impotence.

incontinence

Incontinence is a problem which is generally much more widespread than you might imagine from the coverage it gets in newspapers and magazines, or the extent to which people own up about it. Society may have become more open in some respects, but while it is now possible to advertise sanitary products for women on national television, so far there have been no similar ads for incontinence aids.

Not having full control over your bladder can have a serious affect on your enjoyment of life. Many men admit it impairs their social activities, affects their work, interferes with their sexual relationship and saps their self-confidence. Being incontinent can make you feel ashamed and child-like, anxious and vulnerable. Other people's reactions may reinforce these feelings. However, in order to prevent incontinence ruling your life, you need to find ways of dealing with the way you feel as well as taking practical steps to find solutions to your particular problems.

Owning up to your feelings and facing the reality of your situation is a good start. The next step is to be open and honest with people who are important to you, and also to seek and use outside help so that you can focus on solutions, rather than dwelling on problems.

where to go for help

There are a number of organisations who should be able to offer help and advice. Your health authority may employ a continence advisor, usually a nurse with special training and an interest in incontinence. There may be a local walk-in clinic where you can go for information and advice.

If you can't track down a continence advisor through your doctor or health centre, or you want to talk to someone as soon as possible, call the Continence Foundation national helpline *(see page 92)*. The Continence Foundation is a resource centre and an umbrella group for organisations concerned with continence. They can provide a leaflet on post-prostatectomy incontinence.

Help the Aged has a leaflet on incontinence. Another source of useful information may be one of the Disabled Living Centres which are located throughout the country. The Disabled Living Foundation in London also has a number of useful leaflets *(see page 93 for details)*.

According to the nurses who answer the Continence Foundation helpline, a number of calls come from men suffering from incontinence after a TURP. They are usually concerned that six weeks or so after the operation, they are still experiencing the same kind of urination problems – urgency or frequency, for instance – as they were before treatment.The nurses' first move is to reassure them. As they point out:

"It can take six months to a year for things to settle down and for some men to regain proper control of their bladder." There are, however, some things you can do to help yourself.

self-help
There are a number of different kinds of incontinence. Stress incontinence is the name for what happens when a few drops of urine leak out when you exert yourself physically, lifting heavy weights, sneezing or coughing. It can happen after prostate surgery because the sphincter muscles which hold the bladder outlet shut are a little less efficient after the operation.

A regular routine of pelvic floor exercises may bring about a slow and steady improvement by strengthening and tightening the muscles to prevent this kind of leakage. Some men express surprise at being told that they, like women, have pelvic floor muscles, but these are the ones which support the bladder and the rectum. During urination the pelvic floor muscles relax to reduce the resistance to urine flow.

how to Identify the pelvic floor muscles

If you are not sure where your pelvic floor muscles are, or how to contract them, tighten the ring of muscle around the back passage by imagining you are trying to control the passing of a bowel motion. This will help you identify the back part of the pelvic floor. Don't tense the muscles of your legs, buttocks or tummy while you do this,

To become aware of the front muscles of the pelvic floor, experiment while urinating. Start as usual, then try to stop midflow, drawing up your pelvic floor muscles. (At first you may find you can only slow the stream until you strengthen the muscles through exercise.)

Count to four then start urinating again, making sure you empty your bladder fully. After it is completely empty, tighten up the pelvic floor muscles again for another count of four. Another way of locating the pelvic floor muscles is to cough – this causes the pelvic floor to move outwards.

basic pelvic floor exercise

Now you know where your pelvic floor muscles are, you can practice tightening them regularly to build up their strength. You can do this any time, either sitting, standing, watching television, waiting for a bus. The basic exercise is to contract the muscles, hold for four seconds and then relax. With short rests in between, repeat the cycle at least three or four times. The complete exercise should be done at least twice a day. Try not to hold your breath when doing the exercise. As the muscles get stronger you may be able to do more "pull-ups". More advanced pelvic floor exercises are explained on page 85.

Some people need to continue these exercises for three to six months before incontinence improves, so don't give up if they don't appear to be helping at first.

Urge incontinence is having to rush suddenly to the toilet and not making it in time. It is often accompanied by frequency, the need to pass urine often. Some men also find they are woken up at night by the need to go, some wet the bed while they are asleep. If you had these problems before your operation you may find they persist afterwards, but this does not mean the operation failed. The problems are usually caused by an overactive bladder muscle. While your prostate was enlarged, the bladder had to squeeze very hard to get the urine through the urethra. Post-operatively, the bladder often continues to be overactive and this may take weeks, even months to settle down. Improvement usually occurs within six months to a year. Exercising your pelvic floor muscles will increase the strength of the outlet muscles and make it easier to hang on, on your way to the toilet.

Bladder training may also help. The aim is to learn to suppress or ignore the desire to pass urine, so that you establish a more normal pattern. This means gradually increasing the time between your visits to the toilet so that, by degrees, your bladder becomes able to hold larger quantities of urine comfortably.

Keep a diary or record of how often you pass urine or get wet for two to three days. Look at the pattern and then attempt to hold on, gradually extending the interval between visits to the lavatory.

When you feel the urge to go, tense up your pelvic floor muscles and hold them tight. Cross your legs, or do anything else that helps. Try to focus on something else – say the alphabet backwards or do some mental arithmetic. At first you may only be able to delay your visit to the toilet by a few minutes. You could start by waiting one minute when you feel the urge to go, then five, then 10 minutes.

Don't be discouraged by a few accidents. If you tend to start leaking urine when you hang on, wearing an absorbent pad or drip collector (see below) may give you more confidence. If you stick to your guns you should be rewarded with fewer leaks and longer intervals.

It is not advisable to drink tea or coffee since both contain caffeine which is quite a strong diuretic. If you can't bear to switch to plain water, at least try de-caffeinated brands. But don't cut down on the amount of fluids you drink in the hope that this will help. Your kidneys will still go on producing urine, it will just be very concentrated and this may irritate the bladder which can, in turn, cause incontinence.

You should probably be drinking about 2-3 pints of liquid a day. If you are still having to get up in the night to visit the toilet it is sensible not to drink within about 90 minutes of going to bed, but don't take things to extremes and refuse to drink anything after mid-afternoon.

Some people find it helpful to measure how much urine is passed by using a plastic jug. This can help you to see if your bladder is improving.

Keeping a record throughout the training period will also help you see if progress is being made. The aim is to pass urine only as often as most people – every three to five hours, or five to seven times a day.

Incontinence after passing urine may also be problem. Some find a few drops of urine leak out almost immediately after the bladder has been emptied, or even a few minutes later. This may be because you have not emptied your bladder completely or because urine is getting trapped in the bladder outlet where the prostate used to be. One tip which may help is to sit down rather than stand, and lean forward slightly to pass urine. Some men find that pushing up behind the scrotum and massaging gently helps them expel the last few drops.

making things easier
Incontinence can be made worse if you have problems using the

toilet. Think about steps you could take to make it easier for you. If your only toilet is upstairs it might help to have a commode downstairs, or you could make use of a hand-held urinal. Your clothes may get in the way. You may find loose boxer shorts easier to manage than Y-fronts. Putting an extra tab on a zip may make it easier to open trousers in a hurry, or velcro could be used for flies instead.

continence aids

Incontinence does not always respond to treatment. If yours does not get better with time and self-help measures, ask your doctor to refer you back to a urologist. A few men may be advised to have further surgery.

There are a number of different products to help you manage your incontinence, whether it is temporary or not. By protecting you and your clothing these products can give you the confidence to go out and about without worrying about stains or odour and help you lead a full and normal life. These include:
● Pad and pants designed to be worn under normal clothing
● Penile sheaths, body-worn appliances and dribble pouches. Some are available on prescription from your GP.

There are a number of factors you will want to take into account before purchasing any continence aids. These include:
● Absorbency - how long will it protect you and how often will you have to change?
● Bulk – can it be seen under normal clothing?
● Noise –- does it make a noise before, during or after use?
● Comfort – how comfortable is it to wear
● Ease of use – does it move when you walk or sit, is it easy to change?
● Cost – can your doctor prescribe it for you, or will you have to pay?
● Availability

Some towns have shops or chemists which carry a limited range of products. Boots have their own range of Staydry products, including men's briefs and Y-fronts designed for use with absorbent pads. These should definitely be stocked by the bigger branches and all their branches should stock incontinence pads. The healthcare counter should also have an independent catalogue of products which can be ordered if they are not in stock. Not everyone is comfortable buying or discussing continence aids over the counter but it is also possible to obtain products by mail order. The Continence Foundation can provide help and information and some of the companies offering mail order services are listed at the end of this chapter.

impotence

Some men find they are no longer able to get erections following certain treatments for prostate problems. Urologists often point out that as men get older, erectile difficulties become more common anyway. But whether impotence is incidental to treatment for prostate problems or not, it can be extremely distressing. However, there are a number of effective forms of treatment for impotence.

Not all GPs are familiar with the various treatments that are now available. Some are unsympathetic and some simply find it difficult to discuss such an intimate problem. On the other hand, some GPs are keen to help and may be able to refer you for treatment on the NHS. Either way, it is worth knowing what the options are. The penis contains three spongy chambers which become filled with blood during the arousal stage of lovemaking. As a result. the penis becomes hard, enabling entry into the vagina. For an erection to occur the nerves and blood vessels supplying the penis must be working adequately and a man must be producing sufficient male hormones.

Difficulty in obtaining erections may be caused by a slow inflow of blood into the penis caused by damage to the nerves in and around the penis. Pelvic floor exercises may help in some cases, by reducing the speed of outflow of the blood, so giving more time for blood to accumulate in the penis. Since these exercises can only be beneficial, it would seem wise to try them first before exploring other possibilities.

pelvic floor exercises

The pelvic floor consists of several layers of muscle which support the bladder and the bowel. Men have two openings in the pelvic floor, the anus and the urethra.

Most of the time we use these muscles without consciously thinking about it. We tighten them to control the bladder or the bowel and generally are only aware of them when the bladder or bowel are full. The importance of these muscles for sexual potency in men has only recently been recognised.

For details of how to identify the pelvic floor muscles and do the basic exercises, turn to page 80. *Regaining Potency: The answer to male impotence* by Oliver Gillie also published by Self-Help Direct has full details *(see sources, page 112)*

advanced pelvic floor exercise

After doing the basic exercise several times a day for five days you can move on to a more advanced phase. Contract the muscles of the pelvic floor and hold for four seconds as before, then try to contract them a little more, passing on to a second stage of tightness. Hold this for four seconds and then see if you can tighten once more to a third stage and hold again for four seconds.

Relax completely and rest before repeating the cycle. If the muscles of the pelvic floor begin to tremble, release them and rest before trying the exercise again. Try to keep the muscles of your buttocks, thighs and abdomen relaxed while you tighten the pelvic floor.

The exercises build up strength and potency over time, so do not expect instant results. Benefit may continue to increase over several months if the exercises are continued. The exercises may also be effective when used together with a special vacuum pump or injections.

vacuum pumps and constriction rings

These devices work by drawing blood up into the penis and keeping enough of it there to maintain an erection so that intercourse can take place. A plastic tube is placed over the penis and air withdrawn from the tube, creating a partial vacuum. The negative pressure gradually draws blood up into the penis so that it becomes erect. It generally takes a minute or two (exceptionally up to five) for the penis to become fully engorged with blood. To prevent the blood draining away again a specially designed elastic band is slipped over the base of the penis.

Most men who use this method find that the erection they get reaches much the same length and circumference as a normal erection. Sensation may not be exactly the same, but, even so, it allows satisfying intercourse for both partners.

Different brands of vacuum devices are available and range in price from about £120 to £300. At the upper end of the price range is the Erecaid, which uses a patent elastic ring with grooves on the inside edge. These grooves allow some blood flow during erection. If the ring is accidentally left in position for a long period, the penis will not be damaged through lack of oxygen.

The Erecaid comes with a manually- or battery-operated pump. For suppliers of vacuum pumps and constrictions rings, see the end of this section.

drug treatments for impotence

New drug therapies have revolutionised the treatment of impotence. Injection treatment became widely available in the late 1980s and early 1990s. As a result it was recognised that impotence is often a physical problem and is susceptible to physical treatment. Now further progress is being made with the discovery of new drugs and treatments which produce an erection without any need for an injection.

One of these new treatments, MUSE, is available in the United States and was expected to become available in Britain before the end of 1997. Another drug, Viagra, was expected to become generally available in Britain towards the end of 1998. Other new treatments are expected within two or three years.

Viagra

Viagra is a tablet taken by mouth which may assist erection or make a man more sensitive to sexual arousal. When Viagra becomes available it is likely to become the treatment of first choice for impotence because it is so easy to take. Viagra (chemical name: sildenafil) works by enhancing relaxation of the corpus cavernosa, the cavities in the penis, allowing them to fill with blood in response to sexual stimulation. International scientific trials of Viagra by impotent men have found that it improves the frequency of erections as well the hardness and duration of erection. It enables intercourse to occur more frequently and more reliably in men who are impotent or who are unable to achieve intercourse as frequently as they and their partner wish.

Patients are advised to take Viagra about one hour before intercourse is anticipated. If they have had a heavy, fatty meal, the drug may take longer to work. Alternatively the drug may be taken on a daily basis in order to increase the possibility of a satisfactory erection when sexual excitement occurs. However trials have also shown that Viagra does not increase desire, that is the wish to have intercourse, beyond the normal level. Viagra acts as an enabler, making it easier for men with erectile difficulty to respond sexually.

MUSE (Medicated Urethral System for Erection)

MUSE makes use of an applicator to insert a drug pellet into the urethra. The pellet releases the drug, alprostadil, which dissolves in the small amount of urine left in the penis. The drug is then absorbed into the penis as it is gently massaged. An erection begins within five to 10 minutes of inserting the pellet and generally lasts between 30 to 60 minutes. MUSE can be used twice in 24 hours.

Two thirds of men whose impotence is primarily a physical problem are able to achieve an erection using MUSE in the clinic. However some of these men experience difficulty using the system at home. Your doctor will need to find out the best dosage for you to start on and check that there are no side effects.

In some men MUSE has been found to cause a lowering of blood pressure and fainting. The most serious side effect of MUSE is prolonged rigid erections lasting four to six hours in 0.3% of men using the system and priapism, a rigid erection lasting longer than six hours. These complications occur in a similar frequency with injection treatment. Priapism is treated as a medical emergency. It is relieved by a minor operation to withdraw some blood from the penis. Medical advice should be sought if an erection lasts more than four hours.

A soft rubber constriction ring has been developed for use with MUSE. The ring stops blood from leaving the penis but is not sufficiently tight to stop it from filling with blood. The ring is helpful for men who find that they obtain some response with MUSE but not sufficient to gain a hard or effective erection. MUSE has been developed by Vivus, a US company based in Menlo Park, California, but is being marketed in Britain by another company, Astra.

injections
It is also possible to produce an erection by injecting a drug into the penis. The drugs most commonly used in the past were papaverine and phentolamine. However, these drugs can irritate local tissues and have been associated with fibrosis, small lumps that form near the point of injection. Now many doctors favour the use of prostaglandin E1, sold under the brand name Caverject or Erecnos, because it is not so irritating.

With experience, the dosage of the drug used can be adjusted to produce an erection which generally goes down soon after intercourse. However, there is a small but significant risk of priapism – an erection that lasts longer than is convenient. If an erection lasts longer than four hours there is danger of nerve damage. If this happens, it is advisable to have hospital treatment to reduce the erection by removal of blood.

implants
It is possible to have a plastic rod permanently inserted into the penis to stiffen it. These are called implants or protheses. Several different types are available.

Implants have been shown to work very effectively but now that various types of drug treatment are available, implants are seldom used.

The simplest consists of a plastic rod which bends at the base so the penis can be bent down for concealment and up for intercourse. The penis remains the same length and width all the time, which is a disadvantage.

An alternative is an inflatable implant which makes use of a small pump placed in the scrotum. The pump is worked with finger and thumb, sending fluid into two cylinders in the shaft of the penis. This means the penis increases in girth and there is some evidence that partners find it more satisfying. The implant can be deflated at the press of a button. Even with the inflatable device, the penis stays much the same length when deflated.

In theory, implants are available through the NHS but the fact that the inability to have erections is not life threatening means that operations of this kind are given little or no priority. They are also expensive – the device alone costs £500 – so budgets rarely run to them. Nevertheless, they are available on the NHS from a few specialist centres.

pros and cons
If you are considering treatment for impotence you need to consider how comfortable, convenient and natural a method feels. Some men find injections more natural because once done, intercourse takes place in the normal way, whereas the vacuum method means you have to make love wearing the constriction ring which some men say they find uncomfortable, distracting or embarrassing. On other hand, men who prefer the vacuum method say they like to be able to initiate loveplay without an erection. Another advantage of the vacuum method is that, although it is wise to consult a doctor first and helpful to have a consultation with someone familiar with the use of the method, medical supervision and return visits to the doctor are not necessary.

With injections, bruises commonly appear at the injection site but these are not uncomfortable and do not cause any long term problems. About one in six men report a continuous dull ache in the penis after injection but this pain is not great enough to prevent intercourse in men who are well-motivated.

However, some men say they find it distracting and gave this as their reason for not continuing with this method. Many men dislike the idea of injecting themselves in such a sensitive area, even when they understand that the injection is in the less sensitive shaft of the penis. Some men feel faint or dizzy following the injection – this may be because they are sensitive to the drug or because they are reacting psychologically.

Complications can follow an implant. Sometimes men find them uncomfortable, sometimes infections develop around them, and they have to be removed, sometimes they perforate the skin. With an inflatable device the hydraulics sometimes fail and a second operation is necessary to effect repairs.

Insertion of an implant destroys much of the normal spongy tissue of the penis that acts as a blood reservoir. So normal erections are not usually possible once an implant has been inserted. In general, people report greater satisfaction with injections or vacuum devices than they do with implants, so this should probably be the last option to consider.

A final word of warning: there are some clinics advertising treatments for impotence who canvas by post and offer free consultations, but then demand around £1000 before treatment commences. It is wise to avoid this type of clinic and shop around for medical help at a more affordable price. Any doctor or clinic who offers a cure should be treated with the greatest suspicion.

further information
Suppliers of mail order continence aids:
SCA Molnlycke Ltd, Southfields Road, Dunstable, LU6 3EJ Freephone 0800 393431.

The Tena product range includes pouch pads, which come in two absorbencies. Normal costs £3.84 for a pack of 26, Extra £3.07 for a pack of 18. Reusable cotton pants to hold them in place come in small, medium and large and cost £6.46 each.

Milton Stay-Dry, Granby Court, Weymouth, Dorset, DT4 9XB
Freephone 08801 85108
The Contenta Compleat looks like a normal fly-front pant but has a built-in highly absorbent pad, price £11.65 a pair. The Swan pouch pant also looks like a pair of fly-front pants but has an inside pouch with a leakproof liner and takes reusable or disposable pads. The pouch costs £10.45 a pair and the swan liners cost £10.20 for a pack of 40.
The Silent'n'dry dribble pouch with a waterproof liner has an expanding waistband and can be worn alone or under normal pants. It costs £15.95 for one garment including two liners. Spare liners cost £10.90 for a pack of four. Milton Stay-Dry also sell urinals and pads for protecting bedding and seats.

SimsPortex Kylie and **Kanga** ranges are available via mail order from The Care Shop, Egyptian Mill, Slater Street, Bolton BL1 2HP (01204 384858)
Kylie Male pants are washable. They come in three absorbencies, a range of sizes from 20in to 52in hips, and a choice of three colours, white, grey and black. Prices start from £8 a pair. The Kangamale Marsupial Pants are also washable and designed to be used with pads. They don't have to be removed when the pads are changed. They have a fly opening and traditional Y-front styling, and come in seven sizes fitting up to 60in hips. Prices start from £7 a pair. Kanga Pads come in four different absorbencies and prices start from £2.95 for a pack of 20.

Paul Hartmann Ltd, Unit P2, Parklands, Heywood Distribution Park, Pilsworth Road, Heywood, OL10 2TT
Mail Order Hotline 01706 363244
The wide range of products includes Unitex Sir, washable Y-front styled pants with built-in pads. They come in five sizes from small to XX large and cost £9.98 each.

suppliers of vacuum pumps and constriction rings:
Impower Ltd, 107 The Broadway, Mill Hill, London NW7 3TG
For those men who want a cheap but reliable pump the Impower VTS device can be recommended. Currently it sells for £117.00 + £6.00 p&p.

Osbon Medical (UK), 107 The Broadway, Mill Hill, London NW7 3TG
This company offers a clinical demonstration of all their devices as well as a free telephone counselling service (0181 906 0777). This company is a pioneer in the field and has a reputation for quality pumps through the price range. Several models of pump are available costing from £145.00 +£6.00 p&p to £320.00 + £6.00 p&p for the electrical model. StayErec constriction rings and loading cone are available for £50.00 a set of four rings providing two sizes and two tensions.

Eurosurgical Ltd, Merrow Business Centre, Guildford GU4 7WA 01483 456007
Offers three pumps at prices from £120.00 + £8.65 p&p to £248.00 for a battery operated pump. Their ring constriction device costs £69.00 + p&p, and provides four sizes of rings.

Genesis Medical Ltd, Freepost WD 1242, London NW3 4YR. Helpline: 0171 284 2824.
Impulse pump device, £119.00, requires two hands for operation. Active II pump device £149.00. Asset – a ring constriction device with five rings of different sizes – £24.00

Owen Mumford Ltd, Medical Shop, Freepost, Woodstock, Oxon, OX20 1BR
01993 812021
Provides a rapport VTD pump at £119.00. Recommended by Which, the Consumer's Association magazine, for good value and ease of use. The pump can be operated with one hand but takes a longer time to establish a vacuum than most other pumps. Constriction ring loading system at £19.95 is cheap but only two sizes of ring are offered.

more information from:

Continence Foundation
2 Doughty Street, London WC1N 2PH
Helpline 0191 213 0050
Produces a number of free leaflets. Information available in 10 languages. Books on incontinence are available through the mail order book service. The helpline offers confidential advice from a specialist nurse. Open Mon to Fri 9am to 6pm.

Disabled Living Foundation
380-384 Harrow Road, London W9 2HU
Up to date information and advice on living with a disability. Letters and fax enquiries only (0171 266 2922) or send for leaflets.

Impotence Association
PO Box 10290, London SW17 7ZN (0181 767 7791)
Advice and support to sufferers and their partners. Helpline open 9am to 5pm Mon-Fri, answerphone operates at other times. Send a sae for more information.

SPOD
286 Camden Road, London N7 0BJ (0171 607 8851)
Association to aid sexual and personal relationships of people with a disability.

CHAPTER EIGHT
....

a prostate diet plan

Changing your eating habits may help protect you against the risk of developing problems with your prostate, especially prostate cancer. In Eastern societies, such as China and Japan, where low-fat diets of vegetables and fish are the norm, prostate cancer rates are very low. Plant oestrogens, fibre, antioxidants and zinc all appear to offer protection.

Researchers in New York have discovered that cancerous tumours grow more rapidly in mice fed on a high-fat diet than those on a low-fat one. When the animals on a high fat feeding programme were switched to a low fat regime, tumour growth slowed down.

So what should you be eating?
● **Fat**: We get more than 40 per cent of our calories from fat, much of which is saturated and from animal sources. However, in the East, fat intake is less than 30 per cent and most of that is unsaturated, providing a good supply of essential fatty acids which are vital to prostate health.
● **Plant oestrogens**: Easterners eat higher amounts of phyto-oestrogens which are found in cruciferous plants such as cabbage and Chinese leaves, soya beans, soy flour and tofu. They seem to be sufficiently similar to human oestrogens to counteract the natural male hormones responsible for triggering prostate problems.
● **Antioxidants**: Vegetables and fruit ensure a good supply of antioxidant vitamins, including C,E and the carotene lycopene. These mop up substances which may cause cell mutation.
● **Fibre**: Male hormones which aggravate the prostate are pumped into the digestive tract in bile. Fibre from wholegrain foods, rice, rye and other grains that pass undigested from the body, bond with these hormones and remove them.
● **Zinc**: Diets rich in seeds, nuts and whole grain foods also provide

plenty of this mineral, which appears to control the sensitivity of the prostate to circulating sex hormones.

The aim of a prostate diet plan is to provide a higher proportion of these potentially protective foods. It also aims to provide less than 30 per cent fat, most of which is unsaturated.

● Men of average height – 5ft 10in – weighing no more than 13 stones should aim for 2,500 calories a day.
● Make up any shortfall with wholegrain bread, a medium banana, large apple, pear, orange or glass of fruit juice. To lose weight reduce your calorie intake to 2,000 calories a day.
● You can have up to a pint of skimmed milk in drinks per day.
● Use reduced and low-fat cheeses, yoghurts and spreads
● Eat at least five servings of fruit and vegetables daily. Potatoes do not count – but a glass of fruit or vegetable juice is the equivalent of one serving
● Alcohol in moderation
● You can take a 10mg zinc supplement daily, a general antioxidant and four capsules of rye grass extract such as Prostabrit or a saw palmetto product such as Serenoa-C

The following recipes can be incorporated into your eating plan. The star rating indicates how rich each meal is in helpful substances.
● good
● ● very good
● ● ● excellent

breakfasts
Poached egg on rye:
Toast two slices of rye bread and cut into triangles. Poach an egg and grill two tomato halves. Spread toast lightly with reduced-fat sunflower margarine and top with egg and tomatoes. Serve with a glass of grapefruit juice.
● ● vitamin C
● ● lycopene
● ● fibre
370 calories

Cereal and toast:
45g of Bran Flakes, All-Bran or Start cereal with 200ml skimmed milk. Slice of wholegrain toast with reduced-fat sunflower margarine and marmalade. Coffee or tea with skimmed milk.

● ● ● zinc
● ● ● fibre
390 calories

lunches
Spinach and red pepper Spanish omelette:
Cut half a red pepper in two and de-seed. Grill until charred and blistered. When cool, peel off skin and cut pepper into strips. Heat 1 tsp olive oil and sauté 90g fresh spinach with a clove of crushed garlic. Once wilted, add pepper strips, some chopped parsley and seasoning. Beat two eggs with 2 tbsp skimmed milk and pour over the vegetables. Cook until omelette is set and slightly browned underneath. Finish under a hot grill. Turn onto a plate and allow to cool. Cut into wedges and serve with a chunk of wholemeal or rye bread.

● ● vitamin C
● ● carotene
● zinc
● ● fibre
542 calories

Salmon and broccoli pasta
Cook 50g of wholegrain pasta bows in plenty of boiling water. Drain and cool. Mix with 2 tsps lemon juice and 60g low fat fromage frais, some chopped parsley, salt and black pepper. Toss pasta bows with 50g lightly steamed broccoli florets and 50g canned, flaked salmon. For dessert, serve some stewed blackberries with reduced-fat yoghurt.

● ● ● vitamin C
● ● vitamin E
● ● fibre
500 calories

suppers

Stuffed peppers with honey-roasted sunflower seeds (serves 4)

Cook 700g carrots in 250ml vegetable stock until tender. Grill two red peppers until skin blisters and chars. Cool, then peel off skin and remove seeds. Puree carrots and pepper and add seasoning to taste. Fry 75g shallots for three minutes, add a clove of garlic and cook for one minute. Add puree and a pinch of ground ginger.

Blend one egg yolk with 3 tbsps reduced fat Greek yoghurt. Stir gradually into the pan, don't boil and keep warm. Halve the remaining two peppers and de-seed. Cook in boiling water for three minutes. Drain and fill with the puree. Sprinkle with 2 tbsps honey-roasted sunflower seeds and serve with chunks of wholemeal bread.

● ● ● vitamin C
● ● ● carotene
● ● vitamin E
● ● ● zinc
● ● fibre
373 calories

Tagliatelle with spinach, pine nuts and raisins

Rinse 1.5 kg of spinach and cook for a few minutes in a large pan with no added water, just what is left on the leaves. Drain. Cook 300g wholegrain tagliatelle in a lot of boiling water. Just before it is ready heat 2 tbsps olive oil in a pan. Add three heaped tbsps pine nuts, 100 gms cubed tofu and 1 and half tbsps raisins. Cook for two minutes. Add seasoning and a splash of soy sauce to taste. Serve with the tagliatelli.

● ● vitamin C
● ● vitamin E
● ● ● phyto-oestrogens
● ● zinc
● ● fibre
494 calories

© Amanda Ursell, state registered dietician.

CHAPTER NINE

getting the best out of the system

It would be nice to think that anyone seeking help for prostate problems would get the best treatment available on the NHS, no matter where they lived. Unfortunately, this is not automatically the case: to get the best out of the health system you need to know how it operates, who the key players are and what role you can play in the decision-making which will affect your own health.

Family doctors have always been the first point of contact for the majority of patients. Increasingly, they act as gatekeepers, opening doors so you can see the right NHS consultant and indicating to that consultant the urgency of your case.

But changes within the NHS have also brought about a new emphasis on the concept of shared care: this means that GPs are being encouraged to take a more active role in the diagnosis and management of specific conditions, selecting those cases appropriate for specialist referral while treating others themselves.

There are a number of advantages to a shared-care approach for prostate problems. From the patients' point of view, being treated at the local surgery is usually more convenient and less time-consuming than having to travel to an outpatient clinic at a hospital. A GP knows you and your medical history and, probably, your family and social circumstances. You may find it easier to discuss your problems with a doctor you know. You are more likely to have continuity of treatment and better follow-up. And your GP should be well informed about local services and support groups.

Of course, the shared-care approach has benefits for those working in the NHS, too. There is a shortage, for example, of fully trained urologists, doctors who specialise in disorders of the urinary tract.

The British Association of Urological Surgeons has recommended that there should be one urologist per 100,000 people – a ratio which, in itself, compares poorly with other countries. The figure in 1996 was actually one urologist for every 148,000 people. Even this figure, say leading urologists, hides pockets of very great underprovision.

With not enough urologists to go round – and a population of senior citizens projected to double in the next generation – it is obvious why urologists can make a case for seeing only those patients who really need their services. They argue that this will reduce the number of hospital admissions, cut down the length of time patients have to wait for surgery and allow them to give more time to patients who need specialist care.

They point out that GPs are perfectly capable of diagnosing benign prostatic hyperplasia (BPH) by using a formal scoring system like the International Prostate Symptom Score (IPSS), which was developed under the auspices of the World Health Organisation. They add that various studies and international meetings agreed that only one in five patients with clinical BPH were clear candidates for surgery – which would leave four-fifths of all patients with other options, including medical treatment which might be managed by a GP.

In addition they argue that shared care should increase rather than decrease the early diagnosis of prostate cancer.

Clearly then, your GP will be playing an important role. Even if you are referred to a hospital specialist, and are admitted for treatment, the hospital should keep your doctor informed so that he or she can continue your care.

When you first see your doctor you will obviously want to know what he or she thinks is wrong with you and what treatment they think you will need. GPs are busy people and you may feel that you don't want to take up too much of their time. But it is important to ask for explanations of anything you don't understand. Sometimes it is difficult to take in information when you are worried, so it might help to take someone with you or to make notes. It can also be useful to jot down some questions beforehand. And if later you think of something you wished you'd asked, don't be afraid to make another appointment to get the information you need.

A good GP should answer your questions, discuss the options for treatment, the likely outcome and what side or after-effects the treatment might have. If necessary, he or she should refer you to the clinic or hospital which offers the services you need.

If you are being referred, ask for details. Will you be seen by a general surgeon, a urologist or an oncologist – a cancer specialist? You may want to ask if it will make any difference if you go privately – and how much that would cost.

In the UK, the government has recognised that cancer patients have a right to the care of a cancer specialist, although as yet the intention has not been translated into action. Although, in general, cancer specialists tend to get better results, in 1995 fewer than 50 per cent of all cancer patients were seen by a cancer specialist. The Prostate Cancer Charity recommends that if you are diagnosed as having prostate cancer and are not being seen by an oncologist you should ask your GP to ensure that you are. "We believe that the partnership of oncologist, urologist and GP will ensure that you benefit from the input of all doctors relevant to the treatment of prostate cancer and caring for your general welfare."

Certainly, if you have been diagnosed as having prostate cancer, it makes sense to insist you are referred to a specialist with a recognised interest and expertise in the subject, and to explore all the possibilities before you opt for one treatment over another.

Specialists in prostate cancer – whether urologists or oncologists – understand that choosing between watchful waiting, radiotherapy or surgery, for instance, can be difficult, and should be happy for you to see other specialists, if necessary, before making up your mind.

trials

You may be asked if you are willing to take part in a clinical trial, particularly if you are diagnosed as having prostate cancer. Research into new and better ways of treating cancer is going on all the time and if early work suggests that a new treatment might be more effective than the standard treatment, doctors need to carry out controlled clinical trials to see if this is, indeed, the case. Trials may compare drugs, surgical procedures, radiotherapy and psychological therapies. At the same time, parallel studies may be done to measure the effects of treatment on quality of life.

This type of trial is randomised, which means a computer allocates you at random to one of the treatments being compared. (It has been shown that if a doctor chooses the treatment, or allows the patient to choose, he may unintentionally bias the trial.) When possible the trial is also double blind, which means that neither you nor your doctor know which treatment you are on.

This means that in a randomised controlled trial, some patients will receive the best standard treatment and some will receive the new treatment – which may or may not prove to be better than the standard one.

No-one can force you to take part in a trial and you can drop out at any stage. Your doctor must have your informed consent before starting you on a clinical trial. So he must not only discuss the treatment but explain what the trial is about, why it is being conducted and why you have been invited to take part.

If you choose not to take part, or you withdraw at a later stage, you will then receive the best standard treatment rather than the new one against which it is being compared.

your rights

If you are at all concerned about the treatment you are getting or being offered, it is worth noting that as an NHS patient you are entitled to the following:

● You can change to another GP if, after talking to your current doctor, you are still unhappy with the way you are being treated. You may have to change your health centre. Your local Community Health Centre (Local Health Councils in Scotland and Social Services Councils in Northern Ireland) can advise you on how to go about this and how to make complaints.

● You can ask to be referred to a specialist acceptable to you

● You can ask for a second opinion. It is unlikely that your GP and hospital doctors will all refuse your request but, if they do, you may have to change GP to get the referral you want.

● You should have any proposed treatment and its side effects explained to you.

● You can refuse treatment

● You can see your medical records since November 1991 although doctors can refuse you access if they believe the information in the records would harm you

In an ideal world all GPs would be up to date with the latest thinking on the best ways of diagnosing and treating prostate problems. However, by their very nature GPs are generalists not specialists and you may feel it worth while to look further afield for information or support, if only for reassurance that the advice and/or treatment you are being offered is appropriate.

where to go for more help or information

Prostate Help Association
Langworth, Lincoln, LN3 5DF
Registered charity established to provide essential information to all who suffer from prostate cancer, BPH or prostatitis. For an initial information sheet send two first class stamps. Details of subscriber discounts and the Support Network will be included. Alternatively, send £10 to subscribe to the PHA's Newsletters.

Prostate Research Campaign UK
36, The Drive, Northwood, Middlesex HA6 1HP
Provides information, promotes education and raises funds to finance research into prostate disorders. Send a 9 x 7 inch sae for information and free leaflets. They also publish Prostate Problems-The Facts £5.95

The Patients' Association
8 Guilford Street, London WC1N 1DT
Patient Line 0171 242 3460
Represents the views and interests of patients. Helpline provides advice on rights, access to health services, self-help groups and complaints procedures. Publishes factsheets and self-help guides.

CHAPTER TEN

....

jargon busting

Doctors do their best to explain things to their patients, but not all are gifted with great skills as communicators and it can, in any case, be difficult for someone used to using medical terms automatically to translate these into more easily understood English. The following glossary may be useful.

Adenocarcinoma   The technical name for a cancer of a gland or glandular tissue

Adjuvant therapy   Treatment used with another primary treatment

Alpha blocker   A drug which blocks impulses passing between the alpha receptors of nerves.

Analgesic   Painkiller

Apoptosis   Programmed cell death. The same signal that tells a cell to divide can also tell it to kill itself. Cell division only occurs if that signal is over-ridden by another, confirming the replication process.

Biopsy   Procedure to remove tissue to test for cancer cells

BPH   Benign prostatic hyperplasia – enlarged prostate

Catheter   Thin tube used to withdraw or introduce fluid into the body. A urinary catheter is usually inserted via the urethra into the bladder to drain urine from it.

Cryotherapy   Way of freezing prostate tissue to destroy it

CT   Computerised tomography, a body scan using X-rays and a computer, useful for locating and imaging tumours

Cystogram   A series of X-rays taken following the

	introduction of dye into the bladder. The X-rays are taken as the bladder empties and show any holes in the urethra
Cytoscope	Telescope-like surgical instrument with a light, inserted into the bladder via the urethra. Other instruments can be introduced through it
Detrusor decompensation	Failure of the bladder muscles to contract properly, causing the bladder to become floppy and unable to expel urine
Detrusor instability	Overactivity of the muscular layer of the bladder wall which can cause urinary symptoms such as frequency, urgency, nocturia and urge incontinence
Drain	Tube inserted near a wound to drain away excess blood and fluid
Drip/intravenous infusion	A tube to replace fluid in the body after an operation. One end goes into a vein in the arm, the other is attached to a bag containing a specially balanced saline or sugar solution
DRE	Digital rectal examination
DHT	Dihydrotestosterone, thought to be the main hormone involved in prostate enlargement
EPS	Expressed prostatic secretion, fluid massaged from the prostate
Erectile dysfunction	Failure of the penis to achieve rigid erection; more widely accepted medical term for impotence
Flow Clinic	Urology clinic where various tests are done to investigate the cause of urinary problems
Frequency	The number of times the bladder needs to be emptied
Hesitancy	Difficulty in passing urine which may result in a slow rate of flow
Histology	The study of tissues, used in diagnosis
Hormones	Chemical substances produced by glands which circulate in the blood and help control growth, reproduction and other functions.

Incontinence	An inability to control the muscles which control the passing of urine (or faeces). A loss of bladder control.
Impotence	Failure to attain or maintain an erection firm enough for intercourse
Inoperable	Refers to a cancer that cannot be removed by surgery either because it has spread to nearby organs or because removal might cause too much damage
Irritability	Overactivity of the muscles of the bladder wall causing it to empty at inappropriate times
Keyhole surgery	See laparoscopic surgery
KUB	Kidneys-Ureter-Bladder, X-ray of the area containing these organs
Laparoscopic surgery	Surgery done with the aid of a laparascope, a telescope-like instrument introduced through a small hole to allow the surgeon to examine internal organs. Surgical instruments are inserted through similar small incisions.
Lesion	Any abnormality such as an injury, infection or tumour
Local therapy	Use of treatments such as radiotherapy and surgery which are concentrated on particular areas of the body
Metastasise	Spread of cancerous cells via the bloodstream or lymphatic system beyond the primary cancer site
Metastasis	A secondary cancer at a site distant from the original, primary, cancer (pl metastases)
Microwave therapy	Use of microwave radiation to destroy tissue, can be used to reduce size of obstructive prostate tissue
Micturition	Peeing, the act of passing urine
MRI	Magnetic resonance imaging, a scan using electromagnetism to give high-quality images of organs and structures in the body. Can be

	used to check for cancer spread
MSU	Mid-stream urine, often checked for bacterial infection
Nocturia	Having to get up in the night to pee (often small amounts)
Oncogenes	Cancer causing genes: genes responsible for cell growth and division that, when mutated, may cause uncontrolled cell growth and cancer
Oncologist	Doctor who specialises in the treatment of tumours, particularly cancer
Orchidectomy	Surgical removal of a testis. Bi-lateral orchidectomy is the removal of both
Palliative therapy	Treatment used to alleviate symptoms without curing the condition causing them
Perineum	The area of the body between the scrotum (the pouch which contains the testes) and the anus
Primary tumour	The first (sometimes the only) or the most important tumour
Prognosis	An opinion about the probable course and final outcome of a disease or condition, made when all the facts are known
Prophylaxis	Preventative treatment
Prostatectomy	Surgical removal of part (or all) of the prostate gland
Prosthesis	Artificial device that helps to restore a natural function
PSA	Prostate specific antigen, a substance in the blood. High levels can indicate prostate problems, including cancer
Radical prostatectomy	Removal of the entire prostate by open surgery
Radical treatment	Aggressive treatment aimed at curing a serious illness
Radiotherapy	Use of radiation to kill cancer cells
Regression	Disappearance or reduction of the symptoms and signs of a disease

Retention	The holding back of urine in the bladder due to a blockage or muscular weakness.
Retrograde ejaculation	Passage of sperm back up the urethra into the bladder during ejaculation
Secondaries	Tumours at a site distant from that of the original primary tumour
Staging	Classifying the development of a disease: for example, whether it is localised, has spread regionally or to distant sites in the body. The stage at which a cancer is first detected may affect treatment choices and likely outcomes
Stent	A device which can be inserted into the top of the bladder to relieve obstruction
TRUS	Transrectal ultrasound, an ultrasound scan of the lower abdomen carried out by inserting the scanning device into the rectum
TURP	Transurethral resection of the prostate, a way of coring out the prostate gland via the urethra
TULIP	Transurethral, ultrasound guided, laser induced prostatectomy
Tumour	A swelling or an abnormal growth of cells which can be benign or malignant. Cancer is a malignant tumour.
TUNA	Transurethral needle ablation using radio frequency
TURAPY	Transurethral ablation prostatectomy using radio frequency to destroy prostate tissue
TURF/Thermex	Thermex is the name of a machine which destroys prostate tissue with radio frequency generated heat
Ultrasound	High frequency sound waves are passed through the body. These are bounced back by solid objects so an image of internal organs can be built up by a computer and displayed on a monitor
Ureter	One of two tubes which carry urine from the kidney to the bladder

Urethra	The tube which carries urine from the bladder through the penis. It also carries semen during ejaculation.
Urge incontinence	Leaking urine following a sudden need to urinate
Urgency	Difficulty controlling the sudden need to pass urine
Urinary retention	Inability or difficulty in emptying the bladder
Urinary stasis	The retention of a volume of urine in the bladder after urination
Urine flow test	Measuring the volume and rate of flow as urine is passed into a funnel-shaped container attached to a meter
Urodynamics	Special tests to measure the pressures in the bladder and prostate to discover the cause of urinary symptoms
Urologist	Doctor who specialises in the structure, functioning and disorders of the urinary system
UTI	Urinary tract infection
Vascular	Relating to the heart and blood vessels
WBC	White Blood Count

staging and grading prostate cancer

Staging is a way of assessing the size and spread of prostate cancer. The staging system most commonly used in Europe uses letters and numbers. T stands for tumour, N for node and M for metastasis.

T stages can indicate whether a cancer is still confined to the prostate or beginning to advance locally. N stages indicate the cancer has spread to one or more regional lymph nodes. M stages indicate metastatic problems - the cancer has spread further afield to secondary sites.

For example:

TX	indicates an assessment was not possible
T0	indicates no evidence of cancer
T1	indicates a tumour undetectable except by tissue analysis
T2	indicates a tumour confined to the prostate
T3	indicates a tumour pushing through the capsule of the prostate
T4	indicates a tumour which is invading nearby areas

The addition of the letters a, b or c gives more information. So a T2a tumour is confined to the prostate but involves half a lobe or less, while a T2c tumour, although similarly confined to the prostate, involves both lobes. And while M1 indicates distant metastases, M1b indicates metastases in the bone.

Grading is a way of assessing how aggressive a cancer may be. The Gleason system is the one commonly used. Cancer cells are examined under a microscope to see how they differ from the normal prostate cells in terms of their ability to form gland structures. Clumped-together cells with well-defined edges are less likely to grow rapidly and receive a low Gleason number. Cells distributed randomly with uneven edges are more apt to spread and receive a high Gleason score.

In general, overall Gleason grades of 2, 3 and 4 denote well-differentiated tumours; 5, 6 and 7 denote moderately differentiated; and 8, 9 and 10 poorly differentiated. Some investigators believe that Gleason grade 7 tumours should be classified as poorly differentiated.

Using both staging and grading may help determine the best course of treatment. For instance, an ideal candidate for watchful waiting is a man with a low Gleason score and a stage T1 or T2 tumour.

sources

◆ *Localised prostatic cancer: management and detection issues*, Whitmore WF Jr, Lancet May 1994

◆ *Patient Pictures, Prostatic disease and treatments,* ed Roger S Kirby, 1995 Health Press

◆ *Benign Prostatic Hyperplasia* by Roger S Kirby and John D McConnell, 1995 Health Press

◆ *Shared care for Prostatic Diseases*, Kirby R, Kirby M, Fitzpatrick J, Fitzpatrick A, 1994 Isis Medical Media

◆ *Should We Screen for Prostate Cancer?*, Woolf Steven H, BMJ Vol 314 5 April 1997

◆ *ABC of Urology*, Dawson C, Whitfield H, BMJ Vol 312 Mar 1996

◆ *Prostate cancer, Fact Sheet* May 1996, ICRF

◆ *Our Vision for Cancer*, ICRF 1995

◆ *Prostate Problems:The Facts*, Prostate Research Campaign UK, 1996

◆ *Life After Cancer*, Ann Kent, Ward Lock, 1996

◆ *Men and Cancer*, Cancerlink 1996

◆ *The Cancer Guide*, BBC/Macmillan Relief 1997

◆ *Understanding Cancer of the Prostate*, BACUP revised edition 1995

◆ *A Radiofrequency Method of Thermal Tissue Ablation for BPH*, Bhanot SM, Grigor KM, Hargreave TB, Chisholm GD, Urology Vol 45 No 3, March 1995

♦ *Managing Incontinence*, Cheryle B Gartley, Souvenir Press 1985

♦ *Your Operation: Prostate Problems*, Jane Smith and David Gillatt. Headway, Hodder and Stoughton

♦ *Regaining Potency*, Oliver Gillie, Self Help Direct (new edition) 1997, price £10.95 (p&p free) from Self-Help Direct, PO Box 9035, London N12 8ED

♦ *Current Issues in Cancer: Cancer of the Prostate*, Dearnaley D P, BMJ Vol 308 March 1994

♦ *Drug Therapy: Management of Cancer of the Prostate*, Catalona W J, New England Journal of Medicine, Vol 331 Oct 13 1994

♦ *Cancer Prevention in Primary Care*, Austoker J, BMJ Vol 308 1994

♦ *Prostate Diseases: care and treatment: prostate hypertrophy*, Abrams B, BMJ April 29, 1995

♦ *Prostatitis (Short term Treatment)*, Feliciano AEF Jr, Manila , Philippines: http:www.prostate@mnl.sequel.net

♦ *Sabalin R Product Briefing*, August 1993

♦ *Saw Palmetto: herbal prevention for common male health concerns*, Foster S, Better Nutrition August 1996

♦ *Results of Treatment with Pollen Extract in Chronic Prostatitis and Prostatodynia*, Rigendorff EW, Weidner W, Ebeling L and Bock AC, British Journal of Urology, Vol 71 1993

♦ *Treatment of outflow tract obstruction due to benign prostatic hyperplasia with the pollen extract Cernilton*, Buck AC, Cox R, Rees RWM, Ebeling L. John A, British Journal of Urology Vol 66 1990

♦ *Managing lower urinary tract symptoms in older men*, Abrams P. BMJ April 1995

♦ *Chronic Prostatitis*, A. Doble, British Journal of Urology, 1994, Vol 74, 537-541

Self-Help Direct Publishing

Self-Help Direct Publishing was created by two journalists, Oliver Gillie and Michael Crozier, in 1995 to bring important and useful information direct to the public. It aims to provide people with vital facts about health and other matters, so that they may make crucial decisions for themselves.

We aim to report on the latest medical advances, drugs and treatments for a variety of conditions which may be hard for those not in the medical profession to learn about.

• •

◆ **Oliver Gillie** is a leading medical journalist and author. He was medical correspondent of *The Sunday Times* for 15 years and medical editor of *The Independent* for four years. He has BSc and PhD degrees from Edinburgh University and worked for several years at the National Institute for Medical Research, Mill Hill.

◆ **Susan Aldridge** has a PhD in chemistry and an MSc in biotechnology. Before taking up journalism, she worked for several years as a chemist for the Medical Research Council. Since 1988, she has worked as a freelance journalist and author. She has written three books on genetics and biochemistry. She is medical editor of the monthly science and technology magazine *Focus*.

◆ **Lee Rodwell** is health editor of the popular weekly magazine *Take A Break*. Before becoming a full-time freelance health writer, she was a staff journalist on several national newspapers. She has written many books on health and lifestyle issues and her articles have appeared in magazines and newspapers around the world.

• •

Escape from Pain
◆ New ways to fight back with electronic treatment, age-old remedies rediscovered, psycho-strategy, exercises for mind and body. Conventional and alternative – **Escape From Pain** by Oliver Gillie has something for everyone with pain.

Hair Loss: The Answers
◆ In this book, Dr Susan Aldridge aims to explode a few myths and offer real advice and help for men and women concerned about the loss of hair.

Regaining Potency: The answer to male impotence
◆ Physical love does not have to end with age. This book covers new drugs, new devices to assist, home exercises, and the "food of love" diet – a revolution in understanding and treatment of erection problems. A new fully revised version by Oliver Gillie. Couples need no longer suffer.

Name..
...

Address..
....
....
....POST-
CODE......................................

Please send me ....copy/copies of:

❑ **Regaining Potency** @ £10.95

❑ **Escape from Pain** @ £10.95

❑ **Hair Loss: The Answers** @ £10.95

❑ **You and Your Prostate** @ £10.95

❑ I enclose a cheque/postal order made payable to Self-Help Direct, postage and packing included. *Please allow 21 days for delivery.*

ORDERS TO: **SELF-HELP DIRECT, PO BOX 9035, LONDON, N12 8ED**